A2-Level
Sociology

The Revision Guide

Exam Board: AQA

Editors:
Gemma Hallam, Katherine Reed

Contributors:
Ellen Bowness, Anna Hazeldine, Sean Purcell, Kate Redmond, Neil Renton, Frances Rippin,
Rachel Selway, Emma Singleton, Andrew Walker

Proofreaders:
Sarah Acford-Palmer, Kate Redmond, Jennifer Underwood

Published by Coordination Group Publications Ltd.

ISBN: 978 1 84146 399 5

Groovy website: www.cgpbooks.co.uk
Jolly bits of clipart from CorelDRAW®
Printed by Elanders Hindson Ltd, Newcastle upon Tyne.

Contents

We deliberately haven't put answers in this book — because there are lots of valid ways to answer essay questions. Instead, we've put in a section about how to do well in your exam — which includes a sample exam answer.

The Nature and Distribution of Power

Welcome to Sociology. This first page plunges you straight into the hot topic of Power. As with any topic in Sociology, you have to understand the different views and interpretations that theorists have about it.

Power is about the ability to Control and Influence

The pluralist **RA Dahl (1961)** gives this **definition** of power:
"**A** has **power** over **B** to the extent that s/he can **get B** to **do something** s/he **wouldn't** otherwise have done".

This is a **useful starting point** for understanding power. From this definition of power, you can see that power relationships can involve processes such as **coercion** (**force**), **manipulation**, **bargaining** or **persuasion**. You also need to think about this definition in terms of **society as a whole** and the way that **some social groups** and **institutions** have **power over others**.

Authority is Legitimate Power

Most sociologists agree that there's a **difference** between **power** and **authority**.
Authority suggests a sort of power relationship which is **accepted** by the people who are ruled over —
they give their **consent**. It's useful to remember the phrase "**authority is legitimate power**".

For example, most people obey **traffic lights** when they drive. This isn't because anyone **coerces** us to do it — there's no one standing over us with a gun. It's because we know the **law** says we must stop at a red light, and we recognise the authority of the law, so we obey the law. We give our **consent** to the government that makes laws governing the rules of the road.

Max Weber said there are Three Types of Authority

Weber (1864-1920) was one of the "founding fathers" of sociology.

1)	Charismatic	People give their **consent** to a **charismatic leader** because of the leader's **exceptional qualities**. The leader inspires great **loyalty** and **devotion**. **Religious** leaders are often charismatic. Examples of charismatic leaders might include: Napoleon, Gandhi, Moses and Fidel Castro.
2)	Traditional	People give their **consent** because they **always have**. Established customs and practices are seen as "right" because they've always been that way. For instance, a traditional society might accept their elders as rulers because the elders have always been the rulers of the society.
3)	Rational legal	People give their **consent** to an **impersonal legal framework** (a set of rules). The rules are **rational** because they **make sense** and have a particular and **obvious aim**. A modern example would be stopping at a red light to avoid vehicle crashes.

These types are **ideals** — pure theoretical ideas. Weber suggested that in **real life**, authority could be a **mixture** of the "ideal" types defined above. So in our traffic light example, Jim Random might obey traffic lights because it's part of a **legal system** of understandable rules (rational legal), and because we've **always** obeyed traffic lights (traditional) and partly because he **loves** the Prime Minister (charismatic).

Stephen Lukes has a Radical view — he says there are Three Faces of Power

1)	Decision-making	The power to **make** and **implement decisions** which **affect other people**.
2)	Non decision-making	The power to **set agendas** — i.e. **limit** what's being **discussed**. If a topic isn't even discussed, **no decision** can be made about it.
3)	Shaping desires	The power to manipulate what people **think they want** — powerful groups can make people think they **want** or **consent** to something which actually **harms their interests**.

Lukes suggests that the **third face of power** (shaping desires) is the strongest, because it's never questioned. He suggests that power is exercised **invisibly** by controlling what people **want**. This is related to the ideas of **Habermas** and **Gramsci**. **Habermas** argued that capitalism creates **false needs** — things that people **don't really need**, but **think** they do. **Gramsci** argued that capitalism has a **dominant ideology** which tells people that society is **fair** and capitalism is **best** for everyone.

Karl Marx said only One Group holds power in society — the Bourgeoisie

1) **Karl Marx (1818-1883)** believed that power in society is **finite** (in other words there's only so much of it), and that it can only be held by **one person** or **group** at a time. This view of power is called the **Zero Sum Model**.

2) Marx saw society in terms of social classes **competing** for power. Under capitalism, the **capitalist** class (**bourgeoisie**) hold **all the power** and use it to their advantage and to the detriment of the **working class** (**proletariat**).

3) Marxists tend to reject the idea of authority as legitimate power, suggesting that the working class are **falsely persuaded** to consent to the rule of the capitalist class. He saw authority as just **disguised power**.

4) Marxist sociologist **Miliband (1969)** suggests that **political power** is held by the same class who hold **economic power**.

The Nature and Distribution of Power

Elite Theorists see society as ruled by a small, powerful Elite

1) **Classical elite theorists** like **Vilfredo Pareto (1848-1923)** and **Gaetano Mosca (1858-1941)** saw society as divided between the rulers (**the elite**) and the ruled. The **elite** take all the **important decisions** in society and these decisions are almost always in their **own interest**. So far, they agreed with the Marxist viewpoint.

2) The big difference between elite theorists and Marxists is that the elite theorists thought **elite domination** was **desirable**, **inevitable** and **natural**. They said the elite become the elite because they are **better** than the rest of us. They saw the **rest of society** as a disorganised and apathetic **rabble**. This is **very different to Marxists** who thought that elite domination was unfair and exploitative.

C. Wright Mills introduced the idea of the Power Elite

1) In a more **modern** and **radical** study of the power of elites, **C. Wright Mills (1959)** studied three important institutions in American society — the **business community**, the **military** and the **government**.

2) Mills claimed that the elite in all three institutions formed a **single ruling elite**, which he called the **Power Elite**. Military, industrial and political power were all intertwined in the Power Elite.

3) He concluded that **unelected elites** sharing the same **social background** dominate American society and run economic and foreign policy in their own interests. Mills argued that the power elite **weren't accountable** to the people. He saw **little difference** between American political parties, so no chance to vote for **alternative** policies.

Statistics show the **majority** of British **MPs**, high ranking **civil servants** and **business leaders** come from the same **social** and **educational** background — this phenomenon has been referred to as the "**Establishment**".

In a study of top decision makers, **Lupton and Wilson (1973)** found that connections between them were strengthened by close **marital** and **kinship ties**. Strong internal ties within the elite group make it harder for outsiders to break in.

Functionalists and Pluralists see power as Dispersed through society

1) **Pluralist RA Dahl (1961)** found that instead of one elite group dominating society and hogging all the power, there were actually "**multiple centres of power**" — lots of small groups competing for power. Pluralists believe that all sorts of political parties and interest groups can have **power** over political **decision-making**.

2) **Functionalists** believe that the amount of power in society can **increase** or **decrease** depending on how many people see it as legitimate. This is the **Variable Sum Model**. Pluralists mostly believe the amount of power is **constant**.

3) Pluralists are **criticised** for focusing on only the **first** of Lukes' **faces of power** — the power to make decisions.

Some Postmodernists claim that Power and Politics have Changed

Jean Baudrillard (1983) says that politicians and political parties have **no power** to change the world. All they do is maintain the **illusion** that politics goes on as **normal**. Baudrillard suggests that there's **no real difference** between political parties or politicians and **no real power** — he sees politics as having turned into a **media-driven** system of **signs** with **no hard reality** behind it.

Lyotard (1984) sees postmodernist politics as being about a **loss of faith** in **big political ideologies** that say what society should be like (see p.6-7 for more). Lyotard sees power as belonging to whoever has the most **useful knowledge** — individuals, corporations, governments, etc.

> Baudrillard argues that just about everything has turned into a sea of meaningless images, and that no one can tell what's real any more. Dude...

Practice Questions

Q1 What is the logical difference between power and authority?
Q2 List the three types of authority itemised by Max Weber.
Q3 What are Stephen Lukes' "three faces of power"?
Q4 Explain what is meant by the Zero Sum Model and Variable Sum Model views of power.

Exam Question

Q1 "Authority is legitimate power." Evaluate this view. (40 marks)

Three faces of power, and five mighty morphin power rangers...

... who don't seem to be on the syllabus this year for some reason. Before you can get anywhere with politics, you've got to have an idea of what power is, and who has power in society. Of course, different sociological schools of thought have very different ideas about power. Learn a few names so that you can drop them in your essays — but make sure you keep it relevant.

The Modern State

These pages have definitions and theories about the modern State and its role in society.

Most sociologists **Agree** with **Weber's Definition** of the **Modern State**

According to Weber, the modern State is "a **human commodity** that successfully claims the **monopoly** of the **legitimate** use of **physical force** within a **given territory**".

In other words: ⟹
1) The State is **created by people**.
2) The State can **use force legitimately** — **other** violence in society is **illegitimate**.
3) The State **rules** over a **clear geographical area** — in our case the UK.

The **State** is traditionally made up of **Four Main Institutions**

1) The **government**, who **make laws**.
2) The **Civil Service**, who **implement laws**.

THE STATE

3) The **police**, who **enforce laws**.
4) The **Armed Forces**, who **protect** the **territory** from threats from outside.

Government is often divided into **three branches** — the legislature, the executive and the judiciary.
1) The **legislature passes laws**. In the UK, **Parliament** (House of Commons and House of Lords) is the legislature.
2) The **executive** suggests new laws, and **runs the country**. The executive is often called "the **government**". Confusing.
3) The **judiciary interprets laws**. The **courts** are the judiciary.

In modern times, the State has extended its role into **health care**, **education**, and **nationalised** (state-run) **industries**.

Pluralists see the **Modern State** as a **Neutral Arena** for debate

1) Pluralists see the power of the modern democratic State as **legitimate** and as acting in the interests of society in general. Pluralists see the State as a **neutral arena** where competing interest and pressure groups lobby for **influence** (see p.10). They say the State **arbitrates** (settles arguments) between competing interest groups, but is neutral itself.

2) Pluralists say the modern State is democratic because of the **multi-party system**, and because of the participation of **interest groups** and **pressure groups**. **Dahl (1961)** looked at the role of interest groups in local politics in the USA, and found that **several groups** had influence. An important study by **Hewitt (1974)** shows the **crucial role** of interest groups and pressure groups in **influencing Parliament**. Hewitt said that no one group got its own way all the time.

3) A study by **Grant and Marsh (1977)** showed that business interests in the form of the CBI (Confederation of British Industry) didn't have massive influence over British government policy. A **plurality** of **other interest groups** influenced policy away from what the CBI wanted.

Critics of pluralism claim that **some interest groups** have **more influence** than others. **Marsh and Locksley (1983)** found that the CBI were successful in getting their own way in key decisions (completely the opposite of what Marsh had found in his earlier study with Grant — Sociology is a funny old thing).

Marxists say the **State Supports** the interests of the **Bourgeoisie**

Marx said: "The State is but a committee for managing the affairs of the bourgeoisie."
Marx and **Engels** asserted that the State only became necessary when society became **divided** on the grounds of **class**. They said that in primitive society there were no classes and so no need for a State.

> Engels was Marx's friend and worked with Marx on the Communist Manifesto.

Marxists claim that the role of the modern State is to **maintain**, **preserve** and **perpetuate** the rule of the **capitalist class** over the **workers**. This is achieved in the following ways:

1) **Coercive force** — the **police** are used to contain or suppress **demonstrations** and **riots**.

2) The **illusion of democracy** — universal voting makes it **look** as though everyone has a say and that society is **fair**. This creates the **false consciousness** that the current system is legitimate. However, political parties only represent the interests of **capitalism**, so there's **no real choice**.

3) **Ideology** — a set of ideas by which the State gains approval and consent by persuading people to accept ruling class values. The neo-Marxist **Gramsci (1891-1937)** called this kind of domination **hegemony**. **Gramsci**, **Althusser** and **Poulantzas** all extend the definition of the State to other institutions which pass on values e.g. **churches**, **mass media**, the **family**.

> Althusser called the army, police and courts the <u>Repressive State Apparatus</u>, and the church, family, education and media the <u>Ideological State Apparatus</u>.

Critics say it's **hard to prove** Marxist theory. Concepts like **ideology**, **hegemony** and **false consciousness**, which are key to the Marxist viewpoint, are **difficult to define** and even more **difficult to research**.

The Modern State

Some theorists Criticise the Modern State as being Patriarchal and Racist

1) **Patriarchy** means a social system in which **men have more status and power** than women. Radical feminists view the **State** as a **patriarchal institution** which legitimises and maintains patriarchy.

2) Evidence for this view is that women are **under-represented** at the **top levels of the State** in the UK, e.g. in 2003, only 18% of MPs and 16% of the House of Lords were women, and less than 10% of company directors were women.

3) On the other hand, British society is **much less sexist** than it was 50 years ago, and women now have a **legal right** to **equal pay and opportunities** in the workplace. The feminist **Sylvia Walby (1990)** admits that there have been huge improvements in state policy towards women, but she argues that the State hasn't succeeded in enforcing equal opportunities laws. Walby claims that the State doesn't do enough to **protect** women from patriarchy.

Some people see agencies of the State as **institutionally racist** (see glossary p.72). There's little evidence for blatant racism on the part of the State in the UK, but State policies and attitudes can sometimes **unintentionally disadvantage** ethnic minorities.

Neo-liberals are Opposed to State Intervention in the Economy

1) Neo-liberals argue that the keys to lasting economic prosperity are **individual economic enterprise** and a **market** (economy) which is **free** from **state intervention**. Neo-liberal theorists, like **Hayek (1944)**, argue that state intervention in the economy can **stifle capitalism** and make the economy **less efficient**.

2) Neo-liberals therefore believe that **state interference** in the economy such as high taxes, state ownership (nationalisation), or generous welfare benefits should be **rolled back** (i.e. reduced).

3) The influence of neo-liberal thinking can be seen in the **Conservative governments** of Mrs Thatcher (1979-1990) which **privatised** state industries, **lowered taxation** and **reduced universal benefits**.

4) The **traditional challenge** to the neo-liberal view is the **reformist socialist view** (see p.7). The reformist socialist view is that the State **should intervene** in the economy in order to improve **social welfare** and **equality**. The reformist socialist view is associated with Old Labour, e.g. the post-war Labour government which created the Welfare State.

Third Way theorists want a State with Social Welfare and Capitalist Economics

1) The "**Third Way**" was an idea put forward by the sociologist **Anthony Giddens (1998)** and later adopted by Tony Blair's **New Labour Party**. Giddens has described it as "the modernising left."

2) Third Way theorists argue that the **world is changing**, for example through globalisation, and that **political ideologies** need to **change** and **adapt** as well if they are to remain relevant. The Third Way therefore includes **elements** of **both** traditional **left-wing** (socialist) and **right-wing** (neo-liberal capitalist) approaches.

3) Third Way theory suggests that the **traditional Welfare State** should be **reformed** because it **encourages dependency** (a neo-liberal idea). However, it also argues that the State should reform and manage the **global economy** to such an extent that it is able to **intervene** to **invest in its citizens**, e.g. through **education** and **social policy**. They argue this will **empower the population** to lead more prosperous, healthy and fulfilling lives.

Globalisation has changed the role of the State

1) As part of the process of globalisation (see glossary) **transnational corporations** (**TNCs**) like McDonald's and Coca-Cola have developed and become very powerful economically. **Sklair (1995)** claims that there's a **transnational capital class** who have gained power at the expense of nation states — he claims the State just isn't as important any more.

2) There's a trend towards **internationalisation** of politics, which has reduced the influence of nation states. For example, some important decisions are taken by the **European Union** rather than by its **member states**.

Practice Questions

Q1 Traditionally, what four things make up the State?
Q2 Briefly summarise the Pluralist view on the role of the State.
Q3 Briefly summarise the Marxist view on the role of the State.

Exam Question

Q1 Evaluate the view that the people in positions of most power in society have not been directly elected. (40 marks)

No need to get in a State about it...

There are a lot of strong opinions on these two pages. You need to be able to evaluate these different views fairly and objectively, whatever your own personal opinion. And I bet you do have a personal opinion. If you find yourself taking sides and thinking "stupid liberal do-gooders" or "blimmin' Tories" then take some deep breaths and start again.

Political Ideologies

These pages look at the political ideologies favoured by British political parties.

Conservatism has Three basic Underlying Principles

1) Conservatism emphasises the importance of the **family**, the **nation** and **patriotism** as contributors to **social order** and **harmony.**

2) Conservatism sees people as capable of good and bad — it's suspicious of any ideology which suggests people are either completely **rational** or completely **moral**. Conservatives therefore believe there is a strong need for a **state** and a **legal system** to **control** people and **protect** them from each other.

3) Conservatives believe that **inequalities** between people **occur naturally** and **resist** any attempts to **impose** equality on people.

An ideology is a set of ideas and beliefs about the way things should be.

Three Strands of Conservatism influence the British Conservative Party

Traditional Conservatism wants to keep things as they are

1) This sees society as an **ordered hierarchy** from God downwards and therefore tends to oppose all attempts at change and reform.

2) Traditional Conservatives emphasise **patriotism** and a strong approach to **law and order.**

3) **Traditional** models of **family life** (heterosexual couples where the mother is the primary caregiver) are seen as important. Traditional institutions such as the monarchy and the House of Lords are emphasised as worth protecting.

A Traditional Conservative view of the world influenced the hymn "All Things Bright and Beautiful" — the bit that goes "The rich man in his castle, the poor man at his gate, He made them, high or lowly, and ordered their estate"

One Nation Conservatism (or Paternalistic Conservatism) thinks the government should intervene to help the weak

1) **One Nation Conservatism** was invented in the **19th century** by Conservative Prime Minister and novelist **Benjamin Disraeli.**

2) Disraeli's ideas were a response to the **problems** and **inequalities** introduced by the industrial revolution. He described Britain as **"Two Nations"**, the rich and the poor, which could become **one nation** again if the wealthy would fulfil their **duty** of **looking after** the poor with social reforms.

3) This strand of Conservatism sees a need for some **state intervention** in the economy, to make sure the rich do their bit to care for the poor.

One Nation Conservatism doesn't call for equality. It calls for the privileged to look after the underprivileged in one big happy hierarchical family.

Liberal Conservatism (aka Libertarian Conservatism and the New Right) takes ideas from classical liberalism

1) Classical Liberalism believes in:
   - the **free market** and **free enterprise**
   - **minimal state intervention** in the economy
   - the idea that **individuals** should take **responsibility** for themselves

2) Liberal Conservatism has borrowed all of these ideas.

3) Where liberal conservatives differ from liberals is in their belief in **traditional values** and the need for a **strong state** to regulate behaviour and maintain **social order** and **moral standards.**

This type of Conservatism is most readily associated with Margaret Thatcher. It's also referred to as "New Right Conservatism".

The Conservative Party has had Different Influences through the 20th century

1) Traditional and paternalistic (One Nation) Conservatism influenced Conservative thinking from **1945-1970s.**

2) **New Right Liberal Conservatism** dominated all **Mrs Thatcher's governments** throughout the **1980s.**

3) **John Major's governments** in the **1990s** were more influenced by **One Nation** ideas.

4) Recent Conservative leaders (**Hague**, **Duncan-Smith** and **Howard**) have shifted towards more **traditional** influences. They emphasise **patriotism** and **nationalism** as they oppose the growing power of Europe and the impact of immigration on the UK.

Political Ideologies

Socialists have an Optimistic view of human nature

1) Socialism suggests that human beings are not innately selfish, nasty individuals, but social beings capable of **cooperation**.
2) Socialism aims to work towards **equality**. Socialism is in favour of a strong and generous **welfare state**.
3) In a socialist society, the **state owns and controls industries**. Socialism says they should be run for the **common good**.
4) There are two main strands of Socialist thought – Revolutionary Socialism and Reformist Socialism.

Revolutionary Socialism calls for the violent overthrow of capitalism by the workers

1) This is the socialism of Marx and Engels which sees society in terms of a **class conflict** between the **bourgeoisie** (owners) and the **proletariat** (workers).
2) Marx and Engels argued that working class oppression would become so **bad** that eventually the workers would become **conscious socialists** and organise a **revolution** to establish a classless society.

Reformist Socialism (aka Gradualism or Democratic Socialism) seeks to change capitalism in gradual steps

1) This type of socialism is much more peaceful. Instead of using violent revolution, Reformist socialists stand in **elections** and seek to change society gradually, in stages.
2) **Egalitarian reforms** such as setting up the **National Health Service** in 1945 can be seen as a step in socialist reform. So could the **nationalisation** of key industries by Labour governments in the 1940s and 1950s.

The influence of Socialism on the British Labour Party has Declined greatly

1) The Labour Party was created as the party of the **working class**.
2) It's **never** been a **revolutionary** socialist organisation, but from 1945 through to the 1970s it was heavily influenced by **Reformist** socialist ideology.
3) Since 1979, the Labour Party has gradually changed or removed most of its reformist socialist ideas. During the 1990s, the party redesigned itself as "**New Labour**" under Tony Blair. New Labour talks in terms of a "**Third Way**" between the party's **traditional** ideals and the necessity to **maintain economic growth**.
4) In 1995, The Labour Party dropped Clause Four of its manifesto — the clause that committed them to **state ownership** of industry.

The Liberal Democrats are influenced by Progressive Liberalism

1) **Progressive Liberalism** was a move away from **classical liberalism** (classical liberalism emphasised free markets, individualism and self help, and favoured a laissez-faire approach to the economy).
2) **Progressive liberalism** calls for **state intervention** to provide services like pensions, hospitals and schools.
3) At the same time it's very clear in its championing of **traditional liberal values** of **individual freedom** and **choice**.
4) The Liberal Democrats' own **constitution** puts it like this: "The Liberal Democrats exist to **build** and **safeguard** a free and open society which balances the fundamental values of **liberty**, **equality** and **community**". So, they want to build a society (i.e. intervene to make it the way they want) to promote equality (intervention again), but make it an open society (liberalism) with individual freedom (more liberalism).

Practice Questions

Q1 What do Conservatives believe we need the state for?
Q2 What is One Nation Conservatism?
Q3 What sort of socialism was the Labour Party traditionally associated with?
Q4 What ideology are the Liberal Democrats influenced by?

Exam Question

Q1 Examine the view that "New Labour" is a different political party entirely to "Old Labour". (12 marks)

But why are groups of politicians called parties? (maybe to fool the gullible into joining...)

Don't worry, you don't have to listen to politicians giving speeches and being interviewed if you don't want to. But if you happen to catch a politician on telly or on the radio, ~~put him or her in a glass jar with air holes in the lid~~, keep an ear out for what they're saying — you might well get a hint of one of these ideologies. Best learn the ideologies on these pages so you can recognise them.

Political Participation

People can participate in political action in different ways.

Citizens of a **Representative Democracy** participate through **Political Parties**

1) In a modern representative democracy like the UK, the people vote to **elect representatives** to make decisions on their **behalf**. These representatives (**MPs** in the UK) are accountable to the voters at the next election — they can get voted out.

2) **Belief systems** (represented by political parties, e.g. the Liberal Democrats, Labour, the Conservatives) **compete for power**. People **vote** to decide who has power.

3) Citizens can participate by **supporting** and **voting** for a particular political party that they share beliefs with. They can also **join** that political party — and help out with election campaigns, or become an **activist** (someone who attempts to influence the party's policies).

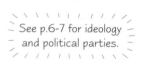
See p.6-7 for ideology and political parties.

Voting Patterns have *Changed*

1) In the **1960s**, people mainly voted according to their **social class**. **Crewe (1983)** found that in the 1964 election, 64% of manual workers voted Labour, and 62% of non-manual workers voted Conservative. The minority of middle class voters who voted Labour, or working class voters who voted Conservative back then were called **deviant voters**.

2) **Crewe (1983)** identified several reasons why working class people switched from Labour to Conservative in the 1980s.
   - **Manual workers** in heavy industry traditionally voted Labour. These industries were in **decline**.
   - There was a "**new working class**" living in the South and working in the service industry and high tech industry. They were mainly owner-occupiers, and no longer identified with **Labour**.
   - **Party image** was increasingly important, and Labour leaders **Foot** and **Kinnock** had **poor public images**.

3) **Marshall (1988)** criticises Crewe, saying that there's **not enough evidence** for the "new working class".

4) **Butler and Kavanagh (1985)** point out that the **1982 Falklands War** was a big factor in **Mrs Thatcher's** popularity, which would explain why people voted Conservative in the 1983 election.

1) Between the **1992** and **1997** elections, the Labour Party **re-positioned themselves** to be more in the **centre** of politics, to appeal to more voters. Under Tony Blair, the party dropped many of their **traditional**, **left-wing** policies and commitments e.g. **democratic socialism**, **nationalisation** and **redistribution of wealth**.

2) In the **1997** General Election, the Labour Party had **strong support** across all socio-economic classes.

3) In the **2005** General Election, **Labour** had **lost** some support among **lower middle class** voters to the **Liberal Democrats**. The **Liberal Democrats** also gained support among **upper middle class** voters from the **Conservatives**. **Labour** lost a lot of support among **students** — the war in Iraq and university tuition fees were unpopular.

Sarlvik and Crewe (1983) say that voting is **less and less based on class**. However, **economic issues** like **tax** are still very important to most voters. **Well off** middle class people are more likely to vote for **lower taxes** than working class people.

"Voter Apathy" is when people *Don't Bother* to vote

Voter apathy is particularly marked amongst the **young** and amongst **ethnic minority** groups. Several measures have been proposed to tackle this apathy. Some have already been adopted.

The postal vote system in the UK has been criticised as open to fraud. Researchers and journalists have shown it's possible to register a postal vote in someone else's name. This accusation has damaged trust in the electoral system.

Already adopted:
1) Making voting **easier** by making it easier to apply for a **postal vote**.
2) Making it easier to **register** to vote — you can register online in some areas.
3) **Educating the voters**, e.g. **Citizenship** is a **National Curriculum** subject in schools.

Not yet adopted:
1) Making **voting** easier by using **new technology** e.g. Internet voting and text message voting. If it's good enough for Pop Idol, it's good enough for choosing our government...
2) Extending polling day to several days.
3) **Redesigning ballot papers** to make them easier to understand.
4) Giving people the option to register a positive abstention — i.e. a box to tick that says "none of the above" or "abstain".

All of the measures appear to focus on the **voters** as the problem rather than the political parties themselves.

Some countries, e.g. Australia have tried to tackle the problem of voter apathy by making **voting compulsory** by law. This has not yet been proposed in Britain.

Political Participation

People also participate in politics through **New Social Movements (NSMs)**

1) New Social Movements are movements which **challenge** the **established political** and **cultural order** in capitalist societies. This includes feminism, environmentalism, anti-racist movements and the global anti-capitalist movement.

2) Most members of NSMs tend to be **young** (mainly between 16 and 30) and **middle class,** particularly from the **public sector middle class** (teachers, social workers, etc).

This includes young people whose parents are teachers, social workers etc.

Direct action happens **Outside** normal **Political Processes**

1) Direct action is political activity which happens outside the normal political processes. It includes **peaceful demonstrations**, **sit-ins** and **boycotts**, as well as violent action such as **riots**, **vandalism** and **terrorism**.

2) Some direct action is **large-scale** and **public**, e.g. **demonstrations** and **marches**. Some is **targeted**, e.g. letter and leaflet campaigns, vandalism and boycotts.

3) **New Social Movements** are far more likely to engage in **direct action** than traditional political activity. They don't have a **strong voice** in party political debate. Members of NSMs often feel they **have to take direct action** in order to get their views on the **mainstream agenda**. Getting noticed by the **media** often plays a big part in this.

4) Direct action can be successful in **persuading governments** to take action, as long as it appears to represent **mainstream public opinion**. A government which doesn't follow mainstream public opinion risks **losing votes** in the next election. It's similar for direct action against businesses — the business will act if it thinks it risks losing sales.

Protests for and against fox hunting involved media, government and class

Anti-hunt:	"Hunt sabotage" is **direct action** against fox hunts aimed at disrupting the hunt so the fox could get away. It had limited impact on public opinion. **Pressure groups** (see p.10) have also campaigned against hunting. Since the 1920s, the League Against Cruel Sports lobbied politicians, and produced publicity material to persuade the public into thinking that fox hunting was wrong. By the late 1990s, **public opinion was largely anti-hunt**.
Government:	In their 1997 and 2001 election manifestos, the Labour Party promised to have a vote in Parliament on a law to restrict or ban fox hunting. During debates in 2003 and 2004, Parliament decided to completely **ban hunting**.
Pro-hunt:	The **Countryside Alliance** organised **pro-hunting protest marches** on London both before and after the debate in Parliament. They claimed that banning hunting would cause job losses in rural areas. This did not reflect **mainstream public opinion**, and their protests were unsuccessful.
Class:	Pro-hunting protesters were seen as **"toffs"** by some sections of the media. Many MPs who voted against hunting were traditional Labour MPs from urban working class constituencies. Some people saw the hunting ban as **"class war"**.

Direct Action is often **Against The Law**

Most illegal direct action is **still peaceful**. **Civil disobedience** means direct action which breaks laws. For instance **mass trespass** is a common form of civil disobedience practised by **anti-motorway protestors** who put themselves physically **in the way** of developers in an attempt to protect woodlands etc.

Some **direct action** is **violent and criminal** and has been characterised as **terrorism**. For example, terrorist direct action has been taken against the **USA** and its allies by anti-American Islamist groups, e.g. Al Qaeda. Terrorism also happens on a smaller scale. For example, some **animal rights groups** send **letter bombs** to scientists involved in testing on animals, **threaten families** of scientists involved in animal testing, put **bricks through windows**, and **fire bomb** shops selling fur goods.

Practice Questions

Q1 What do people vote for in a representative democracy?

Q2 Who are the "new working class" and how do they vote, according to Crewe?

Q3 What is voter apathy? Give two methods used to combat voter apathy.

Q4 Give three examples of types of direct action.

Exam Question

Q1 Examine the view that voting behaviour in the UK is no longer class based. (12 marks)

I vote we stop learning about this and go and watch telly...

No no no that was a joke. Keep learning. Learn I say! Learn! There's a lot to get through on these two pages — you need to know about different kinds of participation — voting and direct action. As tempted as you might be to hold a sit-in at the AQA exam board HQ, it probably won't help your grade. Unlike, let's say, a nice spot of revision. So keep on learning!

Influences on the Political Process

These pages examine the influence of political parties, pressure groups and the mass media on the political process.

The **Influence** of **Political Parties** on the **Political Process** is in **Decline**

1) For many years the UK was seen as the classic model of the **Two Party System** — i.e. a system where two **big**, **powerful** and **distinct** political parties compete for power. Other parties exist in a two party system but they don't have a **realistic chance** of winning an election and forming a government.

2) Sociologists have been writing about the decline of the influence of the main political parties since the 1960s. In this view, the fact that political parties have **fewer members** and **fewer activists** shows that they're **less likely** to **inspire** people to go and **vote**.

There's some powerful evidence that the influence of political parties is in decline:

1) **Party membership** and **activism** is declining among Britain's three major parties. For instance, **Labour Party** membership is currently less than **300 000**, having fallen from a peak of **400 000+** in **1997**. **Conservative Party** membership has fallen from over **1 million** during the time of Mrs Thatcher to fewer than **325 000** today.

2) Young people especially are turning to **New Social Movements** to participate in politics (see p.9), and they are less likely to vote in elections than older people.

However, **Reiter (1989)** is **sceptical** of the claim that political parties are in decline. He says there isn't enough evidence across different countries, and over a long enough period of time.

Neo-Marxist **Martin Jacques (1997)** suggests that because of the decline in political parties, British politics should move away from the "Westminster model", which focuses exclusively on the mainstream parties. Jacques suggests a greater appreciation of new forms of political participation, e.g. direct action and protest.

Ideologically, British **Political Parties** appear to be becoming **Less Distinct**

1) Between 1993 and 1997, New Labour under Tony Blair dropped a lot of traditional socialist policies, in an attempt to win votes among the lower middle classes.

2) Policies on **taxation**, **foreign affairs** and **economic management** have become very **similar** in the **Conservative Party** and the **Labour Party**.

3) **Consensus** (agreement) and **convergence** (coming together of views) between parties happens because all parties are trying to get the "average" person to vote for them. **Extreme** political viewpoints don't win as many votes as **centrist** viewpoints.

4) However, consensus and convergence gives voters **less choice**, which may make them **less bothered** to go and vote in elections.

The candidates debated the only issue they didn't agree on.

Pressure Groups also **Influence Politics**

Pressure groups **lobby** politicians — i.e. they try to persuade them to make decisions that suit the pressure group.

Pressure groups can be either **protective** (also called **sectional**) or **promotional**. **Protective**, or **sectional**, groups seek to protect the interests of a particular group, e.g. trade unions protect groups of workers, the CBI protects the interests of business, and the British Medical Association looks out for doctors. **Promotional** groups promote causes, e.g. Greenpeace and Friends of the Earth promote environmental causes.

Pluralists argue that pressure group activity is an essential feature of modern democracy.

1) Pressure groups give **valuable input** to government policy, and provide expert opinion.

2) Pressure groups provide a vehicle for many **views** to be **represented**.

3) **Pluralists** say pressure groups have **equal access** to government. The state is seen by pluralists as a **neutral arbiter** between different **pressure groups** with different opinions.

See p4 for more about the role of the state as a decision maker, and the influence of pressure groups.

Marxists suggest that pressure group activity doesn't enhance democracy at all.

1) Pressure groups tend **not** to be **democratic**. Members tend to have little say in the running of the group. Pressure groups aren't accountable to the people as a whole, so Marxists don't tend to think they should have power.

2) Pressure groups are **not equal** — some have more resources and therefore much more influence than others. Marxists claim that the most powerful groups are always pro-capitalist ones.

3) Marxists think the state **isn't neutral**, and can't be a neutral arbiter between pressure groups.

Influences on the Political Process

The **UK Mass Media** were **Pro-Conservative** until the **late 1990s**

1) Up until 1997 the only paper that ever expressed consistent support for the Labour Party was the **Daily Mirror**. Most of the other papers tended to support the Conservatives.

2) In the late 1990s "New Labour" made it a **priority** to win the support of **big media owners**, particularly **Rupert Murdoch**. Murdoch's News International controls the **Times**, the **Sun** and **Sky television**.

3) The results can be illustrated by the contrasting ways in which Sun headline writers treated two Labour leaders — Neil Kinnock in 1992 and Tony Blair in 1997. The Sun's 1992 election day headline was "**If Kinnock wins today, will the last person to leave Britain turn off the lights**" (Neil Kinnock was the Labour party leader in 1992, and would have become Prime Minister if Labour had won the 1992 election). The Sun's 1997 election day headline was "**THE SUN BACKS BLAIR — give change a chance**".

4) The support of significant sections of the **mass media** has been cited as a crucial factor in the **continued electoral success** of New Labour. Some of this media support is down to the activities of "**spin doctors**" — party PR officers whose job is to **manipulate** the media and make sure that the party is presented in a sympathetic light, while the party's opponents are presented negatively. Spin doctors came into the public eye with New Labour, but media image was important in politics before that — e.g. **Mrs Thatcher** worked hard to put across her "**Iron Lady**" image.

5) Political parties spend huge amounts of money on **advertising** before a General Election, when it's most important to get their message across to voters, and to present the right kind of **image** to voters.

Marxists suggest that **Media Ownership** makes the media **Pro-Capitalist**

1) Traditional Marxism claims that the media **directly** presents news stories which serve the **interests** of the ruling class, because the media is itself **owned** by the **ruling class**.

2) Neo-Marxists suggest that the world view of the capitalist class is broadcast and reinforced by the mass media through an **indirect approval process**. Editors are from middle class backgrounds, so they tend to select material which reflects their own ideas.

3) **Gramsci's** idea of **ideological hegemony** (see p.4) really applies here. Ruling class values are portrayed through the mass media as natural and common sense. Ideas that question capitalism are ridiculed as crazy.

4) A recent **example** of this was an attack on the policies of the Liberal Democrats by The Sun in which they superimposed Lib Dem leader **Charles Kennedy's face** on the label of a **bottle of whisky** to illustrate an article about the Lib Dems. The headline was "Red Kennedy", suggesting that the Liberal Democrats were **socialists** (red is the colour of socialism), and the subheading was "**Loony left policies of Lib Dems' boozy chief**".

The work of the **GUMG** suggests that **News is Politically Weighted**

The GUMG studied news reports of industrial disputes in the 70s and 80s

Method:	The Glasgow University Media Group studied television news over a long time span to look for evidence of bias. They performed detailed content analysis on television news bulletins.
Finding:	The selection of news was biased in favour of dominant class values. Voice-over scripts were biased in favour of dominant class values. Management had more access to the media than union leaders. Filming and editing were biased in favour of the police.

Spin doctors can **influence** news about politics by presenting the media with "exclusive" **news stories** and **press releases** which show their own party in a good light, and opposing parties in a bad light. Journalists are often grateful for a good story.

Practice Questions

Q1 Explain what is meant by the Two Party System.

Q2 Give three pieces of evidence which suggest that the influence of political parties is in decline.

Q3 Give two examples of ways in which political parties use the media to influence voters.

Exam Question

Q1 Assess the view that the differences between political parties have diminished. (40 marks)

Do you know who Gramsci is? Well do you?

Gramsci (1891-1937) was a Marxist who founded the Italian Communist Party in 1921. He was chucked into prison by the Italian Fascists, who came to power under Mussolini. And while he was in prison, he did an awful lot of writing. There are some nice letters to his sister, and quite a bit of writing about ideology. Anyway, I digress...

Theories of Religion

Sociologists disagree about religion. Some think it's great and stops society descending into chaos, others think it's just there to oppress people. God doesn't seem to have much to do with it.

Marx said Religion helps to Oppress Workers and Inhibits Social Change

1) Karl Marx said that in **capitalist** society there was a **conflict of interests** between the **ruling class** and the **working class** because the ruling class **exploit** the working class to get the most profit out of them.

2) But — there's **something stopping** the working class from **uniting** and **overthrowing** the ruling class. Marx says the working class are in a state of **false consciousness**. This means they're **not aware** of **how unfair** society is.

3) This is where **religion** comes in. Marx is **very critical** of religion. He says it **keeps** the working class in a state of **false consciousness**. He said, "**Religion is the opium of the people**". This means that it **dulls the pain** of oppression like **opium** — a **drug** which kills pain. It doesn't take the oppression away, though.

> **Marx said that religion justifies social inequality**
>
> 1) People have **the afterlife to look forward** to if they're **good**, so they **don't break the rules** and don't challenge the capitalist system.
>
> 2) Religion **consoles** people with the **promise of life after death** and so they **put up** with their **suffering** here **on Earth** more easily.
>
> 3) Religion often tells people that their **position is decided by God**. This encourages false consciousness by blaming God instead of **blaming capitalism**.
>
> 4) If **God is all powerful** he could **do something** about the suffering **if he wanted to**. He **doesn't** do anything — so people think this must be **how society is meant to be**.

Marxism says that religion **passes on beliefs** that **oppress the working class**. It argues that religion is a **conservative** force which prevents revolution — it keeps things the same. The **rich stay rich** and the **poor** keep on working. It's a **neat social control**.

But... there are problems with applying this Marxist view to today's society. Fewer people go to a place of worship than in the past — if people **don't go to worship**, it's **hard** for them to be duped by formal religious ideology. Also, religion can bring about **change**, but Marxists tend to ignore this.

Functionalists see religion as Maintaining Harmony and Social Cohesion

Functionalists also see religion as something that **inhibits change** and helps **keep society as it is**. But they think this is a positive role, which creates **social order** based on **value consensus**.

1) **Durkheim** studied **Aboriginal** society and found that the **sacred worship of totems** was equivalent to **worshipping society itself**. Durkheim said that sacred religious worship encourages shared values.

2) **Malinowski (1954)** looked at how religion deals with situations of **emotional stress** that **threaten social order**. Unpredictable or stressful events like births and deaths create **disruption**. Religion **manages these tensions** and **recreates stability**.

Religions have ceremonies for dealing with birth and death.

3) **Parsons** wrote in the 1930s and 1940s that religion provides **guidelines** for human action in terms of "**core values**". Religion helps to **integrate** people into a value consensus and allows them to **make sense of their lives**.

4) Functionalist **Bellah (1967)** suggested the idea of **Civil Religion**, which is when secular (non-religious) symbols and rituals create **social cohesion** in a similar way to religion. **Flags**, famous **political figures** and even **royal deaths** bring about some kind of **collective feeling** that generates **order** and **stability**.

> Functionalism ignores **dysfunctional** and **divisive** aspects of religion. There are **religious conflicts** all over the world. Religion can be a source of **oppression**. Religion can also bring about **change**, and Functionalism ignores that as well.

But in some cases Religion can Encourage Social Change

1) Marx's good pal **Engels** reckoned that in **some circumstances** religion could actually be a **revolutionary** force. Sometimes **religion** is the **only means of change** because all other routes have been blocked.

2) **Early Christian sects** opposed Roman rule and brought about change. **Jesus** himself encouraged social change.

3) In the 1960s and 1970s, **Catholic priests** in **Latin America** criticised the bourgeoisie and preached **liberation theology** — using religion to free people from oppression. This led to **resistance** and **social change** — in 1979, revolutionaries threw out the oppressive government in **Nicaragua**. Neo-Marxist **Otto Maduro (1982)** studied liberation theology. He said religion is "often one of the main available channels to bring about a social revolution".

4) Reverend **Martin Luther King** and the **Southern Baptist Church** resisted oppression and segregation, bringing about **political** and **social rights** for black people in **1960s America**.

5) In Iran, **Islamic fundamentalism** encouraged **social change**. In 1979, there was a **revolution** against the Shah, led by followers of the Shia ayatollah **Ruhollah Khomeini**. Khomeini set up a **religious government** that followed Sharia law.

Theories of Religion

Weber said that Religion can Create a Capitalist Work Ethic

Weber's book *The Protestant Work Ethic and Spirit of Capitalism* looked at how the **religious** ideas of **Calvinism** brought about social change. Weber spotted **two important things** in Calvinism:

1) **Predestination:** This is the idea that your **life** and whether you're going to heaven are **predetermined** by God. Calvinists believed only a **few** were **chosen** for heaven. This created **anxiety** — no one knew if they were chosen.

2) **Ascetic Ideal: Working hard** in your job was a **solution** to this anxiety. Success might be a sign that you were chosen for heaven. Early Calvinists lived a **strict** and **disciplined** life of hard work and simple pleasures.

Weber claimed that the ascetic ideal helped create an ethic of **disciplined hard work**. This is the **spirit of capitalism**. Not only was there a build-up of **capital**, there was the right **work ethic** for capitalism. Religion **indirectly** brought about change.

However — **Eisenstadt (1967)** contradicts Weber's theory by claiming that capitalism occurred in **Catholic** countries like Italy **before** the **Protestant Reformation happened** and before the ideas of **Calvin ever came out**.

Feminists point out the Sexism in Religion

However, <u>menstruation</u> is seen as <u>taboo</u> in many religions.

1) Women's capacity to **have babies** gives women an **important role** within religion, in terms of bringing **new life** into the world. Women's role as **primary caregiver** is seen as **important** by traditional religion — it's the job of a mother to raise her children to **believe in God** and worship God. Feminists say this **traps** women in **traditional** roles.

2) Because women are **sexually attractive** to men they're perceived to be **distractions** from worship. Many religions believe in giving worship to God through a denial of sexuality (e.g. priests in the Roman Catholic Church have to be **celibate**). Religions have historically seen women as "**temptresses**" of men — think of Eve and the apple.

3) Women are **excluded from power** in many religious organisations — for example, the Roman Catholic religion doesn't allow female **priests**, and the Muslim religion doesn't allow female **imams**.

4) Feminists argue that religious texts **transmit messages** to readers through stories that reflect and uphold a **patriarchal** society. This patriarchal ideology says that women are part of the profane and imperfect, and maintains **conformity** and the **submission** of women.

profane = opposite of sacred or holy

5) **Simone de Beauvoir (1953)** saw religion as **exploitative** and **oppressive** towards women. She thought that religion promotes the idea that if women **suffer** in their present lives, then they'll receive **equality in heaven**, which allows women to **put up with** being treated as **inferior** to men in the hope of gaining in the afterlife. Spot the **similarity** to **Marx's** ideas on religion — just swap "women" for "working class" and you're there.

There are Problems with Feminist Anti-Religious Views

1) Women are not necessarily **passive victims** of religious oppression. Women may **actively resist** oppression — e.g. in **Afghanistan** under the Taliban it was forbidden for girls to go to school, so women educated girls in secret.

2) Religion **isn't necessarily patriarchal**. For example, **veiling** can have **positive functions** for Muslim women. The veil can **affirm Muslim identity** and **protect** women from sexual harassment in public.

3) Patriarchy within a society may be transmitted by other social and cultural activities, not by religion.

For Postmodernists there's No Universality in religion

Lyotard (1984) discarded all **metanarratives** (stories about how the world is and should be) **including religion**.

Postmodernists **reject universal truths**, and the postmodernist view of religion favours a **pick and mix** approach to belief.

Practice Questions

Q1 In what ways does Marx say religion justifies social inequality?

Q2 What is the role of religion, according to Functionalists?

Q3 What two aspects of Calvinism favoured a strong work ethic, according to Weber?

Q4 Give three examples of feminist views of sexism in religion.

Exam Question

Q1 Evaluate the view that there is sexism in religion. (40 marks)

The function of religion is to give you someone to pray to before exams...

There's an awful lot to learn here, I'll be honest. To make it easy on yourself, take each kind of theory individually. Once you've read it through, what Marxists and Functionalists think about religion ought to be no big surprise. The next step is to learn the key names and studies. Cover up each subsection and work on it until you can remember the names and ideas.

Religious Organisations

Religious groups organise themselves into different forms. They differ in leadership, relationship to the state and politics, how they worship and who they appeal to. Sociologists have put forward different classifications of religious organisations.

A **Church** is a **Well Established Religious Organisation**

Social historian **Ernst Troeltsch (1912)** distinguished between different kinds of religious organisation, and used the word **church** to mean a **large religious organisation**. He said churches usually have four main features:

1) A church claims **monopoly over the truth** — it says its claims are **absolutely true** and others are **false**.

2) Churches have a **complex rigid hierarchy** and a **bureaucratic structure** with lots of **rules and regulations**.

3) Churches often have a **close relationship** to the **State**. Some nations have an official national religion — Weber used the term "**ecclesia**" for this.

4) Churches are closely integrated into **mainstream society**. Churches act as a **conservative** force, resisting change. This is why the **upper classes** are more likely to join — even though churches are **universal** and **inclusive in principle**.

Examples of churches include the **Roman Catholic Church**, the **Church of England** or the **Episcopalian Church**.

Troeltsch studied churches in **16th century** Europe. **Steve Bruce (1995)** says that Troeltsch's points don't always apply to churches any more because there's **religious pluralism** these days. The Church of England doesn't claim a monopoly over the truth and it isn't always conservative.

Religious pluralism = lots of different types of religious groups.

Sects are **Small, Radical Religious Movements**

Troeltsch defined sects as being almost the **opposite of churches**. Few religious groups fall into the category of sect.

People who are **dissatisfied** with mainstream religion can be attracted to a sect. Sects are often formed by people **splitting off from a church** because they **disagree** with the church's **practices** or **theology**.

1) Sects claim a **monopoly over the truth** and are intolerant towards other religious organisations.

2) Sects have **no complex hierarchy**. They often have a **charismatic leader** who **persuades** members to **follow his / her teaching**.

3) Sects are **small**. Their members follow with **total commitment**, and they can be **manipulated** by the sect's leader.

4) Sects are separate from the state — they're in **opposition** to mainstream society. Sects can sometimes offer an alternative way of life for **deprived** and **marginal** groups.

Examples of sects include **early Methodists** and **Calvinists** (although over time these have become more mainstream). This category also includes **extremist** groups like the **People's Temple** in America who were led to mass suicide by Jim Jones, or the **Branch Davidians** led by David Koresh.

These extremist groups are generally called cults in everyday language. Watch out though — in sociology, cult means something else (see below).

Denominations are **Subsets** of **Churches**

Troeltsch **originally classified** religious organisations into **churches** and **sects**. The term "**denomination**" was added later.

1) Denominations don't usually claim **a monopoly over the truth**. They see themselves as a **possible route to the truth**. They are **tolerant** towards other religious organisations.

2) Like a church, they have a **hierarchy** and **bureaucratic structure** but it isn't as complex.

3) They have a reasonably **large membership**, but not as large as an established church.

4) Members of denominations are usually **not as loyal** as members of churches.

5) Denominations **aren't closely connected** to the State but they do get involved in society and **comment** on **current events**.

Examples of denominations are **modern Methodists** and **Baptists**.

This is only one definition — cults are sometimes defined as movements offering a 'new path to salvation'.

Cults are **Mystic Movements**

Bruce (1995) defined cults as movements without a fixed set of beliefs. They emphasise the **inner power** of the **individual** and **mysticism**. Cults are usually loosely knit and don't have a hierarchy.

Religious Organisations

New Religious Movements can be Affirming, Rejecting or Accommodating

The term **New Religious Movement** (or NRM for short) includes a **huge range of movements** from diverse sources. They've increased significantly since the 1960s. They don't always fit the old church-sect-denomination-cult divisions. Sociologist **Roy Wallis (1984)** identified three types of new religious movement:

World-rejecting movements cut themselves off from society — similar to sects

1) World-rejecting movements are very **critical** of wider society and are often in conflict with the State.
2) **The Unification Church**, better known as the **'Moonies'**, is one example of a world-rejecting movement.
3) World-rejecting movements require **total commitment**. They demand **significant lifestyle changes.** Members often turn away from family and friends — world-rejecting movements have developed a reputation for **"brainwashing"** members. It's often hard to leave a world-rejecting movement.

World-affirming movements are tolerant of other beliefs — similar to cults

1) They're similar to **self-help** and therapy groups — they try to **"unlock spiritual power"**. **Transcendental Meditation** is an example of a world-affirming movement.
2) World affirming movements seek **wide membership**.
3) World-affirming movements **don't require** especially high levels of **commitment**.

These terms tend to be used differently by different people — there aren't clear-cut definitions.

World-accommodating movements are traditionally religious — similar to denominations

1) World-accommodating movements often come from **traditional** religions.
2) They try to rediscover **spiritual purity** lost in traditional religions. **Pentecostalism** is a movement within Christianity that aims to bring the Holy Spirit back into worship.
3) World-accommodating movements allow people to carry on with their **existing lifestyle**.

New Age Movements are a type of New Religious Movement

1) **New Age Movements** are close to cults and world affirming movements. New Age ideas often aren't linked to an organisation, but spread through a culture. Examples include **dowsing, feng shui, crystals, neo-paganism** and **Reiki**.
2) **Heelas (1996)** claims that New Age beliefs are dedicated to **"self-spirituality"** and the development of the self.
3) **Bruce (1995)** highlights **three themes** to New Age Movements: **New Science** rejects many claims of traditional science, **New Ecology** is concerned for the environment and **New Psychology** sees the self as sacred.
4) New Age appeals to **women** more than men and **middle class** more than working class.

Millenarian Movements believe in Salvation through a Cataclysmic Event

Millenarian movements claim that members will achieve **salvation** through a **cataclysmic** event — a major disaster. Millenarianism is connected to **apocalypticism** which believes that **divine forces** will **overthrow** the existing social order. Millenarian movements are associated with **deprived groups** or areas where there has been **radical social change**.

Practice Questions

Q1 Give two characteristics of a church.
Q2 Give two characteristics of a sect.
Q3 Name the three kinds of NRM identified by Wallis, and give an example of each.
Q4 What are the three New Age themes identified by Bruce?

Exam Question

Q1 Identify and explain two differences between churches and sects. (8 marks)

Not just a building with a steeple, then...

Classifying religious organisations is really hard. Some religious groups don't fit easily into these categories — or they might fit into more than one category. Another thing to watch out for is that Sociologists sometimes disagree about how to define terms, especially "cult" and "NRM". Learn the definitions on these pages — but remember that you might come across alternatives.

Religious Organisations

People join religious organisations for different reasons. Lots of them probably believe in God, but they do so in different ways.

The Growth of New Religious Movements isn't easy to explain

The **interactionist** (also known as **interpretivist**) idea is that **new religious movements (NRMs)** provide **certainty** in times of **uncertainty**. When there's uncertainty, new religious movements have **greater appeal** and **grow** in numbers. **Weber** set out three kinds of **uncertainties** that cause people to turn to religion:

1) **Marginality** — inequality, immigration and racism may **marginalise** some groups. So, some new religious movements may help marginalised people **make sense** of their situation, and may promise a better life after death as **compensation**. Theologians call this the "**theodicy of disprivilege**".

2) **Relative deprivation** — the concept of marginality doesn't explain why **white, middle class groups** join new religious movements. According to **Glock and Stark (1965)**, some middle class people may see themselves as **deprived in comparison to their peers**, though they aren't absolutely deprived.

3) **Social change** — transformation of society can result in **uncertainty** and **anomie** (a state of moral confusion in society caused by an absence of shared norms and values). The breakdown of **community**, the process of **secularisation** (see p.20), **cultural diversity** and bad news such as **terrorist attacks** may generate uncertainty.

Modernity and postmodernity create uncertainty. Some sociologists believe industrialisation causes **alienation**, increased bureaucracy and disillusionment with work, which creates **uncertainty**. Postmodernity and the choice people have in constructing their identity may create **uncertainty** and a **crisis of identity**.

Melton (1993) didn't agree that NRMs emerged in periods of uncertainty. He looked at the founding dates of non-conventional religious organisations in the US. **Rapid growth** took place in the **1950s** — in a period of **stability** and **certainty**. Why do these sociologists never agree...

Wallis (1984) Explains the Appeal of the Three Kinds of NRM

1) **World-rejecting movements** grew in numbers in the 1960s. There was a lot of **freedom** for people, but also **uncertainty**. It was a period of **radicalism** with lots of alternative world views — often called the "sixties counter-culture". Wallis argues that some people got **disillusioned** with this counter-culture and wanted more **concrete** beliefs.

2) Wallis claimed that **world-affirming movements** develop as a means of coping with a **crisis of identity** in more successful groups (e.g. the middle class). They try to unlock **human potential** and help people solve their problems. **Bruce (1995)** claims that they're a response to the **rationalisation** of the modern world where it's hard to find satisfaction from work.

Some people find uniformity strangely comforting...

3) **World-accommodating movements** appeal to those who are dissatisfied with existing religion, but still maintain similar beliefs and disciplines.

New Age Movements appeal to people already Examining their ~~Navels~~ Identity

1) New Age beliefs appeal to people who have **turned away from traditional religion**. New Age beliefs say that people can find salvation, peace or perfection **inside themselves**. They often appeal to **middle class** people working in "**expressive professions**" — actors, writers, social workers, counsellors, therapists etc.

2) New Age Movements help some people cope with the **uncertainties** of modernity. In the modern world, people have a lot of **different roles**. New Age beliefs can help people find a sense of **identity**.

3) New Age movements may also reflect a **cultural change** in mainstream society. People are surrounded by non-conventional religious ideas like horoscopes, feng shui and self-help books. **Mass communication** gives us an awareness of different movements. In a **postmodern** society of **choice** and **diversity**, people can **pick and mix** from all kinds of New Age philosophies to help them construct their own identity.

Some Religious Movements attract people who Desire Social Change

1) Sects and denominations often attract people who want **social change**. People **turn away** from the **established church** because they feel it isn't acting in their **interests**.

2) This doesn't always have the intended aim. **Halevy (1927)** claimed that **Methodism** prevented revolution in the 19th Century. Dissatisfied workers turned away from the established state church to find enlightenment with the Methodists. Although they **changed religion**, they **kept on working**.

Religious Organisations

Niebuhr believed Sects were Short-lived

Niebuhr (1929) argued that sects wouldn't survive beyond one generation. They'd either mellow into denominations, or disappear completely.

This idea is known as 'death or denomination'.

1) Sects rely on a **charismatic leader**. If the leader **dies**, the group can often no longer hold itself together.

2) A problem arises when the **second generation** are born into a new sect. They didn't decide to join the sect so they sometimes don't follow with the same religious fervour.

3) Some people join only in times of crisis and leave when the crisis is over. If a sect **demands change** in society and the change actually comes about, the sect **isn't needed any more**.

4) It's difficult to **maintain extreme teachings** and **totally reject society**. A sect can survive if its ideologies become **less rejecting** and **more accommodating**. Sects can eventually become **denominations.**

> The **Methodists** are a good example of this. As the Methodist movement became **upwardly mobile** in the **19th century**, its members **modified their beliefs** in order to make them more **socially acceptable**. The strict **disciplines** of the sect were **relaxed**, and it gradually became a **denomination**.

Some sects **deliberately destroy themselves** — e.g. Jim Jones' People's Temple, and the Heaven's Gate sect.

Others are **destroyed by society** and law-enforcement agencies — e.g. David Koresh's Branch Davidian sect.

Modern culture is fast-changing anyway — sects aren't immune from the tendency to be easy-come, easy-go.

Wilson argued that Some Sects could survive as Sects

1) **Wilson (1970)** argued that **Conversionist** sects are likely to mellow into denominations. Evangelical sects can still convert people and "save souls" whether they're a sect or denomination.

2) Wilson classified **Introversionist** sects as separate from the world, and claimed they therefore can't become denominations. The Amish, Shakers and Mennonites are Christian introversionist sects. Amish and Mennonites have a fairly high degree of second generation retention. Shakers, on the other hand, are celibate, so need to attract new believers or risk dying out as Niebuhr predicted.

3) **Adventist** sects are classified by Wilson as waiting for the **end of the world**, or the **second coming of Christ**. The whole point of adventist sects is to separate from the world in preparation for the end, so becoming a denomination is not an option.

> **Wallis (1984)** thought that a **world-affirming sect** could survive by changing its emphasis, in order to **maximise** its **appeal**. For example, the **Transcendental Meditation** (TM) sect started out as very **spiritual**, then identified with **1960s counterculture** (the Beatles were visitors to the TM ashram in India). In the 1970s and 1980s, TM aimed to sell itself to new believers on the strength of **material gains** that it claimed could be had via meditation.
>
> World-affirming movements like TM can change quite easily. They can also develop a small **core** of **committed** believers, almost like world-rejecting movements.

Practice Questions

Q1 Give three sources of uncertainty which cause people to turn to religion.

Q2 Which kind of NRM appeals to successful people undergoing a crisis of identity?

Q3 Give three reasons that Niebuhr suggests for sects disappearing after one generation.

Q4 Which kind of sects are most likely to turn into a denomination, according to Wilson?

Exam Question

Q1 Assess the view that sects and cults are short-lived. (40 marks)

Lots of religions don't condone sects before marriage...

Different religious movements are always going to appeal to different people. I mean, a middle aged Protestant looking for a more exciting church is probably going to go for something different than a tofu-eating reflexologist looking for something to bring out their inner goddess. Sects and cults tend to market themselves, and even change their beliefs to appeal to more "customers".

Religion and Social Groups

Gender, age and ethnicity are all factors affecting religious participation levels. You're least likely to participate if you're a young, white, working class male, and most likely if you're an elderly, Asian, middle class female. But it's really up to you.

Religious Participation varies by Age

Age affects how religious people are.

1) People **under 15** and **over 65** are more likely to be involved in religious activity. However, participation by those under 15 usually takes the form of **Sunday school** and **religious playgroups**.

2) The **over 65** group is the **most religious** in terms of **belief**. They aren't necessarily the most likely to practice their religion by going to church, because of difficulty with mobility.

3) However, some recent studies claim that the **elderly** are **increasingly losing faith** in God.

4) **Middle aged** groups are more likely to get involved in **world-affirming movements**.

5) **Sects** and **cults** are more likely to be populated with **young adults**.

- **Sects** often appeal to young adults by messages of **friendship** and **companionship** — this can be attractive to those who are experiencing forms of **anomie** (lack of social/moral standards) and **detachment** from the world, and those who have few responsibilities (e.g. they're single, no children).

- **Cults** appeal to the **inner thoughts** and **feelings** of young adults who are often alienated from the primary cultures of society. **Cults** are attractive to individuals who are often already engaging in **counter culture** activity.

6) Young adults may be less religious than older people because of the way that society is changing. An increase in **rationalisation** means there's less **need** for religion to explain things.

This is linked to secularisation — see p.20-21

Religious Participation varies by Gender

1) **Women** are **more likely to attend church**, and more likely to say they belong to a religion (British Social Attitudes Survey, 1991). This has traditionally been explained by women's traditional role as **primary caregiver**. Going to **church** and **raising children** to be **religious** is traditionally seen as an **extension** of that role.

2) **Differential socialisation** is also a factor. The argument goes that girls are socialised to be **passive** and to **conform** — which fits in with the behaviour of more **traditional** and **conservative** religious groups.

3) Another argument is that **women** simply **live longer**. More women are on their **own** as they get older, and they may **turn to religion** for a sense of community. **Older** people are **more religious anyway**.

4) More **men** than **women** have **turned away** from organised religion in the 20th century.

Remember **de Beauvoir's ideas** about women suffering in the here and now, and believing they'll get their **reward in heaven**. This can be used to explain women being more religious than men.

Women often have Significant roles in New Religious Movements (NRMs)

1) Women generally **participate** in **sects** more than men.

2) Also, many sects and NRMS were **established** by **women**, e.g. the Seventh Day Adventists were founded by Ellen White, and the Christian Science movement was founded by Mary Barker Eddy.

3) **Glock and Stark (1965)** have argued that the gender difference in membership of NRMs is because **deprivation** (social, physical and mental) is **disproportionately** experienced by **women**.

4) **Bruce (1995)** suggests that men are interested in NRMs that advocate **esoteric knowledge**, whereas women are interested in subjects that can be classified as **New Science**, **New Ecology** and **New Spirituality**.

5) Some sociologists claim that New Age movements appeal to women, because they emphasise "feminine" characteristics such as healing, caring and cooperation.

Remember, some NRMs have **narrow beliefs** about **women's role** in society, and therefore may **not appeal** to women. Some new evangelical right wing Christian movements believe that women should not work outside the home. This view is shared by the Nation of Islam.

The Nation of Islam is a religious and political organisation founded in the USA in the 1930s.

Religion and Social Groups

Religious Participation Varies by Ethnicity

The 1994 PSI Fourth Survey of Ethnic minorities (**Tariq Modood et al,** published **1997**) found that, in England and Wales, **ethnic minority groups** are **more religious** and participate more in religion than white groups.

1) Religion maintains a sense of **community** and **cultural identity** within ethnic minority groups.

2) **Johal (1998)** claims that in a multi-faith society such as the UK, **religious identity** has become of key importance to members of ethnic minorities.

3) **Davie (1994)** argued that identification with a **religious organisation** was important to Indians, Pakistanis and Bangladeshis in the UK because it gave a **sense of cultural identity** and a feeling of **belonging**.

- **Modood** found that Pakistani and Bangladeshi Muslims in the UK identified themselves primarily as **Muslim**.
- Many young Muslims have a deeper **knowledge of Islam** than their **parents** do.
- Many Muslim girls feel more **liberated** by wearing headscarves and dressing modestly because they are not subjected to the same **stereotypes** and values as non-Muslim girls.

i.e. rather than British, Pakistani, or Bangladeshi

4) Afro-Caribbean identity is largely based on **ethnicity** rather than religion. However, the **Rastafarian** movement is a religious and political movement in which black identity is key — it's based around **resistance to racism**.

1) **Afro-Caribbeans**, who are mainly Christian, attempted to incorporate themselves into the established churches of the UK but found **racism** within many congregations. One way to tackle this was to develop their own churches and ways of worshipping — e.g. Pentecostal churches.

2) **South Asians**, however, had to establish their faith in a country with **radically different** systems of belief. Religion acted as a **support mechanism** for new immigrants, allowing them to share their culture. South Asians **quickly established** religious organisations — mosques, Sikh gurdwaras, etc. **Bruce (2002)** calls this **Cultural Transition**.

Modood (1994) and **Saeed (1999)** found some evidence for a decline in religious practice among Asians in the UK.

Religious Participation Varies by Class

1) The **middle class** is disproportionately **Anglican** and **Quaker** compared with a more **Roman Catholic** or **Methodist** working class (this can be partly explained due to their popularity in Victorian industrial areas). These results can be seen across many countries such as the U.S. and this would seem to back up Marx and Weber's opinions on Protestantism and capitalism.

2) Religious participation is greater in the **middle classes**, partly because religious affiliation is seen as a **desirable** social characteristic. Church is an opportunity for **social networking**.

3) Some argue that participation in **denominations** and **sects** is based on **class position**, claiming that there are middle class denominations and working class denominations.

4) **Bruce (1995)** found that cults are primarily middle class — in his opinion because they fulfil spiritual needs for people who have little financial pressure.

Practice Questions

Q1 Why do young adults participate more in sects and cults?
Q2 What role does religion play in upholding patriarchy according to feminists?
Q3 Why do middle class people participate more in cults?

Exam Questions

Q1 What are the arguments for and against the view that women are oppressed by religion? (12 marks)

Q2 Critically evaluate the argument that religion continues to have an important role in the lives of ethnic minorities in the UK today. (40 marks)

"Ah no, this is the women's church. Men's church is next door"...

Well, obviously it's not quite like that. The examiners will expect you to know how religion relates to age, gender, ethnicity and class, and also how religious participation relates to those things. You should mention a few studies too — no, don't kid yourself that you can remember them all — what did Glock and Stark argue? What was Johal's study about? Davie's? Saeed's? Ha!

Secularisation

There's an argument among sociologists about whether the world (and the UK) is getting less religious, or not.

Secularisation is when Religion Loses Its Influence over society

Bryan Wilson (1966) defined secularisation as a **"process whereby religion loses its influence over the various spheres of social life"**. Secularisation is said to be a result of the social changes brought about by **modern, urban, industrial society**.

1) **Auguste Comte** claimed that **science** was the **final stage** in the **development of human thought**. He said modern society would be dominated by **science** and not religion.

2) **Max Weber** believed that **modern society** would be the age of **technology**, **rationality** and **bureaucracy**. He said rationality and efficiency **sweeps away magic**, **myth** and **tradition**.

Church Attendance and Membership is in Decline

Source: UK Christian Handbook: Religious Trends 1988/99

Counting bums on pews gives **supporting evidence for secularisation**:

1) **UK church membership** and **attendance** has gone down — **attendance** has fallen by almost 1 million in the last 20 years.

2) Attendance at ceremonies such as **baptisms** and **marriages** has also dropped. **27%** of babies in the UK were baptised in 1993 compared to **65%** in 1900.

Percentage of adult population who go to church

Year	Percentage
1980	10.2%
1985	9.3%
1990	9.0%
1995	8.1%
2000	7.7%

Measuring secularisation by counting **bums on pews** has **limitations**:

1) People may **attend church** but **not believe in God**. They might attend a service, baptism or wedding out of friendship for the people involved, for respectability or because of family duty. Or even to get their kids into a certain school.

2) **Davie (1994)** pointed out that people may **not attend church** because of their **lifestyle** but they do still believe in God. The 2001 Census found that 72% of the population identified themselves as Christians. **Davie** claims that **belonging** to a church and **believing** in religion have become increasingly **separated**.

3) To make comparisons with the past you have to use **old statistics**, which may not be reliable.

Pluralism gives people Choice

Religious pluralism is about **diversity** in types of religious organisations and beliefs in society.
As a result the **established**, **national church loses its influence** in integrating people into **shared values**.
Multicultural societies are more likely to have religious pluralism.

Some sociologists use pluralism as evidence against secularisation

1) The increase in **New Age movements** since the 1980s can be seen as evidence that the **sacred** is becoming **important** again — this is called **resacrilisation**, by the way.

2) **Glock and Bellah (1976)** argue that pluralism is evidence of religion being **transformed**. It shows a trend towards **individuation** — people being free to sample different belief systems to find their **own religious meanings** (this is often called **"spiritual shopping"**).

Wilson and Bruce use pluralism as supporting evidence for secularisation

1) Pluralism gives people **choice**. People might feel freer to choose to **reject religion altogether**.

2) Although some people in modern society have joined **new religious movements**, they are still a **small proportion** of the population. Some sociologists claim the **growth** in NRMs has been **overestimated**.

Desacrilisation is where Religion or Spirituality is Less of a Force in Society

1) Weber thought that magic and myth become less important in modern society. Similarly, **Bruce (1995)** sees **science** and rationality as **undermining religion**. We demand pills when we're ill and use science to explain natural disasters.

2) **Berger and Luckman (1971)** claim that the supernatural or religion used to be necessary to **explain our problems**, but we now see **science** as **more plausible**.

3) However, the **death** of a loved one, **injustice**, **natural disasters** and **terrorist atrocities** still sometimes lead people to prayer and faith in the supernatural. Modern science **can't explain everything** to everyone's satisfaction.

4) **Postmodernists** claim that we've moved **beyond scientific** rationality and we now **mistrust science**.

5) Belief in **astrology** and **lucky charms** and **fanatical interest** in magical fantasy like **Harry Potter** and **Lord of the Rings** demonstrates that people still have an interest in **magic**, **myth** and the **irrational**.

Secularisation

Some *Religious Institutions* have become *Secularised*

1) **Secularisation** of **religious institutions** is when the church becomes **less religious** in its beliefs to **fit in** with the rest of **society**. For example, many churches will now allow divorced people to marry.

2) American sociologist **Herberg (1956)** thinks church attendance shows **commitment to community** and not religion — people go to church to **meet up with friends** and feel like a **part of something**.

3) Remember that **not all religious institutions** have become more **secular**. There is a trend towards **fundamentalism**. The **New Christian Right** in the USA are against divorce, homosexuality and pre-marital sex.

The *Church* may have *Lost Some Functions* and become *Disengaged*

Differentiation is where **society becomes more specialised** so each **institution** in society has **fewer functions** than in the past. For example, the **church** used to have an important **educational** function. But since the 19th century, more separate institutions have developed for this role and state involvement has increased.

According to **Bruce (1995)**, religion becomes **less important** in society as some of its previous functions are taken over. **Wilson** says that religion has little influence, and is only involved in symbolic "**hatching**, **matching** and **dispatching**" rites.

Disengagement is when the church is **separated from the State**.

1) According to Bruce, religion has **less influence** as a result.

2) **Parsons (1974)** claims that although the church may have lost its functions and become disengaged from the state and politics, religion can still be **significant in everyday life** and encourage **shared values** in society.

3) Religion is still closely linked to **politics** in the **Middle East** and **Northern Ireland**.

Secularisation is very *Difficult* to *Measure*

There's more about sociological research methods in Section 4.

1) There are lots of different **measures of secularisation**. Some are more valid and reliable than others. **Surveys** show **high levels of religiosity**, but **quantitative measurements** of **church attendance** are **low**. **Different religious groups** measure membership in **different ways**, anyhow.

2) The term **secularisation** is a general term that's sometimes applied just to Christianity. It's important to know **what's being measured** — the decline of **religion in general** or the decline in **Christianity** in particular.

3) It's difficult to measure and make comparisons because sociologists use **different definitions of religion**. Some sociologists use **substantive definitions** which say **what religion is** — e.g. "religion is belief in the sacred". Some sociologists use **functional definitions** saying **what religion is for** — e.g. "religion is for creating value consensus".

4) Functional, inclusive definitions of religion include a lot more institutions than the traditional religions. **Luckmann (1967)** claims that **Marxism** is a religion, because it's a human attempt to make sense of our place in the universe.

5) To measure whether society has become **more secular** you have to compare it to **the past**. Some sociologists argue that we tend to see the past as a **golden age** of religion where **everyone** believed — which is **far too simplified**.

6) Research into secularisation can also be rather **ethnocentric** — focusing on **Christianity** and what the **predominantly white British mainstream** does. Islam, Hinduism and Sikhism are also changing and developing in different ways.

Practice Questions

Q1 How did Bryan Wilson define secularisation?

Q2 How does religious pluralism support secularisation?

Q3 What is meant by desacrilisation?

Q4 Define the term disengagement.

Q5 Give one reason why it can be difficult to measure the importance of religion.

Exam Question

Q1 "The UK is now a secular society." Evaluate this view in the light of sociological argument and evidence. (40 marks)

So, science is the new God, and religion is just *so* last season...

Or maybe not. The sociologists just can't seem to agree. Fewer people are going to church, but that might not necessarily mean that they've stopped believing in God. And pluralism and NRMs — some sociologists use these as evidence in favour of secularisation, while others use them as evidence against. I think they all need to stop squabbling, apologise and shake hands.

Development and Underdevelopment

There are different ways of defining and measuring development and underdevelopment, and tons of theories to explain why some countries are more developed than others.

Development is **Defined** in **Different Ways**

1) Development is usually used to mean economic growth, industrialisation, and high living standards, e.g. high life expectancy and universal education. Countries which have achieved this are called **MEDCs** (More Economically Developed Countries). Countries which haven't are called **LEDCs** (Less Economically Developed Countries).

2) This definition is **ethnocentric**. It defines development in terms of "Western" ideals — which may not be 100% valid.

3) **Undeveloped** countries aren't developed **yet**. **Underdeveloped** countries haven't developed as much as other countries with the same resources.

GNP = economic value of goods and services produced by a country over a year.

Development is **Measured** in **Different Ways**

1) Capitalists argue that **economic indicators** such as **Gross National Product** (**GNP**) are the only effective ways of defining a country's potential for developing (along capitalist lines).

2) However, GNP doesn't tell you how wealth is **distributed**. In a country with a high GNP per capita (per person) there may be a **minority** living in **deprivation**.

3) Economic indicators also ignore **externalities** caused by economic progress — e.g. pollution.

4) Some claim development is better measured by **social factors**. They measure development using **lists** of **basic human needs** — e.g. the Human Development Index (HDI), Human Poverty Index (HPI) and Personal Quality of Life Index (PQLI). Unlike economic indicators, these can show that there is deprivation even in "developed" countries.

All **Development Theories** have their foundations in **Marx**, **Durkheim** and **Weber**

1) **Marx** said that capitalism and industrialisation were about obtaining the **maximum** amount of **profit**. Capitalists in developed countries **exploit** underdeveloped countries to get **raw materials**, and to get a wide **market** for the goods produced by capitalism. Marx thought that capitalism would give way to **communism**.

2) **Durkheim** argued that societies would **progress** through **industrialisation** and that the most developed nations were those which had industrialised first. Durkheim saw the West as the most advanced society, and thought underdeveloped countries could improve their progression by taking on the **characteristics** of Western countries.

3) **Weber** argued that society was becoming more **rational** and **bureaucratic** — people needed to make more choices and come up with new, scientific ideas to solve social problems like deprivation. Less developed societies would need to copy Western **attitudes** in order to allow progress and economic development.

Modernisation Theory says countries **Progress** towards **Liberal Capitalism**

Modernisation theory says that **all countries** move **towards liberal capitalism**. Undeveloped countries are seen as **inferior** to **developed** countries that have achieved a higher rate of **production**, **consumption** and **wealth**.

Rostow (1971) suggested that all countries go through a five stage process of development:

1) Basic, **agricultural** society.

2) **Transition**, or preparing for "take off" — farmers produce a surplus and make money from selling cash crops. Small towns develop, and there's some industry on a very small scale.

3) **Industrialisation** or "take off" — rapid growth of manufacturing. People move from rural to urban areas.

4) **Drive to Maturity** — lots of investment, and the right social conditions for growth. Large cities develop.

5) **Mass consumption**, or "developed economy" — wealth spreads, people buy more and the service sector grows.

The explanation for poverty and underdevelopment is insufficient agricultural surplus to fund investment, insufficient investment in technology, and not enough hard working business people to create opportunities.

Kerr (1962) focused on **cultural factors** — he believed that countries need Western style politics and social values in order to develop, and they should replace traditional culture with Western values.

Neo-liberalism believes in using **Free Trade** to help countries **Develop**

1) Neo-liberalism says that government intervention **distorts** the natural economic processes of the **free market**.

2) Neo-liberals such as **Friedman (1962)** believe in using **free market trade** to help the development of countries. Neo-liberalism is favoured and pushed by the International Monetary Fund and the World Bank.

3) They point to **Newly Industrialised Countries** (NICs) such as the "**Tiger Economies**" to prove that removing tariffs (charges for importing and exporting) and encouraging free trade can lead to development. "Tiger Economies" are South East Asian Countries such as Singapore and Hong Kong that have experienced a period of growth over the last 20 years.

Development and Underdevelopment

Modernisation Theory and Neo-liberalism are both criticised

Both are criticised for being **ethnocentric** (arguing for the superiority of Western culture and industrialisation), and critics say this leads them to distort the true history of Western involvement in developing countries.

Neo-liberals and modernisation theorists also argue that Western methods of development are easily imitated and likely to succeed — which isn't necessarily true. In fact, the Tiger Economies got into serious economic trouble in 1997 after attempting to **extend too far** and **too fast**.

Dependency Theory says Developed countries Exploit Underdeveloped ones

1) **Dependency theory** was a reaction **against modernisation theory**. The key dependency theorist is **Frank (1967)**.

2) Dependency theory says that developed countries **exploited** underdeveloped nations during colonial times (esp. the 19th C.) when they controlled them as part of an **empire** (see p.24-25), and prevented them from industrialising.

3) When the underdeveloped nations got political independence, they were often still **economically dependent** upon their former imperial rulers. The poor nation's main trading partner is often its former colonial ruler.

4) The theory says richer developed nations organise trading relationships in their favour. They set the price for goods.

5) **Dependency theory** is **Marxist** — it argues that **workers** in the poorest nations are **exploited** by the **ruling class**. They're paid very low wages, so the profits from the goods they make and grow go to the ruling class. Developed nations pay a low market price for the goods, and sell the goods in the developed nation for a profit.

6) The theory goes on to say that profits pass from **workers** in **satellite areas** (less developed agricultural areas), to the **ruling class** in the **metropolis** (big cities — former outposts of colonial power), and out to the **developed nations**.

The theory doesn't fully define what development is or give realistic suggestions for how it can be resolved. It also doesn't explain why **socialism also exploited** and created dependency — e.g. the Eastern European satellite states depended on Russia. Dependency theory is criticised for being **deterministic** — it assumes that **everyone in LEDCs** will be **exploited**, and it doesn't accept that some LEDCs might **choose** capitalism, instead of being pushed into it.

World Systems theory says there's one global economy

1) **Wallerstein (1974)** suggested World Systems theory, which treats the entire world as one economy, rather than looking at development country by country. World Systems theory divides the world into **core** (developed countries), **semi-periphery** (e.g. South Africa, Mexico) and **periphery** (e.g. Ethiopia).

2) According to the theory, **core** countries make **full use** of the global economy, and can affect any other country — in other words, they have a global "**reach**". Core countries are the ones which get the most out of capitalism. The core takes up all the surplus profits generated by the whole world — periphery and semi-periphery countries.

3) World Systems theory says the **semi-periphery** countries are **exploited** by the core countries, but they also **exploit** the **periphery** countries. In the theory, because they exploit as well as being exploited, they aren't fully "on the same side" as the periphery countries — no unity amongst the exploited means no united action to change the system.

This theory is also criticised for being too **deterministic**. It doesn't allow for **individual countries' characteristics**, and it still holds up the **core countries** as the model for perfect development.

Practice Questions

Q1 What are the five stages of development according to Rostow?
Q2 What is the central idea of dependency theory?
Q3 What is World Systems theory?

Exam Questions

Q1 Compare and contrast Dependency theory and World Systems theory as explanations of underdevelopment. (40 marks)

Q2 "Modernisation theory is the only accurate way of defining development".
Assess arguments for and against this view. (40 marks)

Singapore and Hong Kong have stripy economies that go 'RAAAR'...

And they go stalking through the jungle, swishing their tails... or they would, if they weren't just boring old economies. Quick point — don't use the terms "first world", "second world" and "third world" — the second world doesn't exist any more after the fall of Communism. Pages 24-25 will help with all this — they give some of the historical background to colonialism, and its effects on trade.

Relationships Between Societies

This fine pair of pages is about colonialism, international trade, and globalisation. Globalisation has economic, political and cultural aspects. No, don't switch off, this really isn't that boring. Honestly. Look, there's a photo of a burger and everything.

The **History** of **Colonialism** has shaped **International Trade Relations**

1) A colony is a territory that's **controlled** by a **foreign power**. Back in the 16th and 17th centuries, **European** countries began to **colonise Asian**, **African** and **American** territories. The height of colonialism was in the **19th century**.

2) European nations colonised foreign territories for three main reasons:

- Colonies were **economically important**. **Raw materials** and **food** were sourced in the colonies, and taken back to Western Europe to fuel **industrial-capitalist development**.

- Having **colonies** and building up an **empire** added to a nation's **power** and **influence** — the colonising country could put military bases and trading ports in the colony.

- Europeans also saw colonialism as a way of **"civilising"** native people. They saw traditional Asian, African and American cultures as **inferior**, and tried to **replace** them with Western values, including Christianity.

3) Colonialism strongly shaped **economic development** in the colonies. The colonisers set up plantations to grow **cash crops** such as coffee and cotton. They used slave labour and low-paid labour and sold the crops for high prices in the European market.

4) Former colonies are often **under-industrialised**, because they were used only for primary sector industries such as agriculture and mining. Former colonies didn't get the chance to develop **manufacturing** industry.

5) Former colonies which rely on **agricultural exports** are hit hard by **global recession** — when the **market price** of cash crops drops, their **national income drops**.

Globalisation has resulted in a Global Economy as well as National Economies

Giddens notes that **technological change** has transformed the way people live — global **communication** and **travel** are now easy. Goods can be **transported** across the world, and **information** can be transferred across the world **instantaneously**.

1) **Globalists** (sociologists who believe that society is becoming globalised) argue that **international trade** and investment have caused national economies to blend together into a **global economy**.

2) **Trans National Corporations** (**TNCs**) operate across national boundaries. They tend to have their headquarters in MEDCs and set up production in countries where there's **cheaper labour**, in order to maximise their profits.

3) **Fröbel et al (1980)** first referred to the **New International Division of Labour** — manufacturing tends to be done in developing countries, and knowledge-intensive work is done in MEDCs. **International division of labour** also means that **different stages of production** can be done in **different countries** — the car industry is a good example.

4) **TNCs** have a **positive** effect — they bring **jobs** and **investment** to developing countries, which can help with their national strategy for development. There's also a benefit for **international consumers** — cheap consumer goods.

5) However, some argue that this is a new form of **exploitation**. **Neo-Marxist** critics of globalisation say that the people of the developing world are turned into **"wage slaves"** for the capitalist system.

6) TNCs aim to create **global markets** for the goods they manufacture. They affect cultures throughout the world.

7) **TNCs** also have an effect on the **business culture** of host nations. TNCs can be categorised as three types — **ethnocentric** (headquarters in country of origin runs everything and sets corporate culture), **polycentric** (managed locally, according to guidelines set by headquarters) or **geocentric** (management is integrated across all countries).

Weberian sociologist Ritzer (1993) writes about global standardisation and "rationalisation".

1) He refers to a **"McDonaldisation"** of production across the world. He says products are made with the same values as a **fast food** outlet: the product is made in **assembly line** conditions, it must be **inexpensive** to make and must be **standardised** at all times, across all the countries where it's made and sold. A Big Mac is the same everywhere.

2) Ritzer picks out five themes within this McDonaldisation — **efficiency**, **calculability**, **predictability**, increased **control**, and the replacement of **human** workers by **machines**.

There's also Globalisation in Politics

1) Politics is increasingly carried out on an **international** level, rather than a national level.

2) The United Nations is responsible for enforcing international law, and peacekeeping etc.

3) There's increased **international political cooperation** — e.g. the **European Union**.

4) **International** non-governmental organisations (**NGOs**) coordinate **aid** and **campaigning**.

Sweet, juicy global standardisation.

Relationships Between Societies

Increased Communication spreads Cultural Goods across the world

1) The increase in **international media** communication in the last few decades has meant that cultures that were once local have become international and global. British and American pop music is everywhere. American and Indian films are seen internationally.

cultural goods = films, clothes, food, music, books etc.

2) Postmodernists argue that this allows people to consume a **plurality** of cultures. They think that globalisation leads to **hybridity** (a **pick and mix** of cultures) rather than one culture being imposed over another.

3) Critics point to the concentration of the **production** of cultural goods in the hands of a few large **TNCs** which have a lot of power in developing countries. They fear that TNCs will replace traditional culture with Western culture to try and **create new markets** for **Western cultural goods**. Critics refer to cultural globalisation as **cultural imperialism**.

4) Those who believe in the **positive** effects of cultural globalisation argue that it's a **two way process**. Western culture is transmitted to new societies, and other identities and cultures get passed on to societies in MEDCs. An example of this would be the increase in screenings of **Bollywood films** in Western mainstream cinemas.

Global Organisations are seen by some as More Powerful than Governments

1) TNCs operate in **many countries** — they have a global reach. Many are as powerful as nation states in economic terms, and some critics point to their perceived lack of respect for local cultures as a key feature of globalisation.

2) National governments often find it hard to **control** TNCs and are **reluctant** to act against the interest of the TNC. The host nation **risks losing large numbers of jobs** if the TNC decides to pack up and **move to another country**.

3) **International political agencies**, such as the **United Nations** and the **European Union (EU)**, have taken some power and decision-making away from national governments.

4) Critics claim that this means nation states lose the ability to **determine their own future**, as they must constantly **negotiate** with other governments and agencies to try and get the best policy for the nation.

Leslie Sklair (2000) sees globalisation as a form of **transnational capitalism** (capitalism which crosses national boundaries). He thinks it isn't worth analysing nation states — power is held by TNCs, bureaucrats and global media.

There's Evidence to say that the role of the Nation is still as Important as ever

1) **Realists** point out that **national interest** still determines **most policies** within a nation and in international negotiations. For example, the US refuses to sign up to the Kyoto Protocol (an international environmental strategy) **partly** because it's not in the interests of the US because of the potential effects on employment.

2) **Hall (1995)** argues that in a global world, **national identity** becomes very **important** to people as a way of ensuring there are still differences between the countries of the world. As a result, the nation state can be strengthened.

3) Increasing fears over the loss of power from national government to the EU has meant that many people in the UK are ever more determined to protect the **sovereignty** of the nation.

4) There's a trend towards **devolution** — i.e. giving power to local bodies, e.g. the Scottish Parliament and Welsh assembly. Nations **within** the UK have reasserted their identity and control over key issues and policies.

Practice Questions

Q1 Explain the three main reasons why European nations colonised foreign territories.

Q2 What is the New International Division of Labour?

Q3 What is "McDonaldisation"?

Q4 Why do critics of cultural globalisation refer to it as cultural imperialism?

Exam Questions

Q1	What are the arguments for and against the view that we live in a 'McWorld'?	(12 marks)
Q2	Critically evaluate the argument that economic globalisation benefits less developed societies.	(40 marks)
Q3	"Despite globalisation, identity, culture and power are held by local communities and nation states rather than international organisations and agencies." Explore the arguments for and against this statement.	(40 marks)

So the world is turning into McDonald's? I reckon Ritzer was just hungry...

Hallucinations and bizarre fantasies are common during extreme hunger. But seriously, globalisation is a big thing in Sociology. Giddens is obsessed by it. It's a many armed beast, is globalisation. It's got cultural, technological, political and economic aspects. Pretty much everything we buy has some kind of global connection. Think of how much stuff has 'made in China' stamped on it.

Strategies for Development

There are different sociological perspectives on development strategies. And unfortunately, you have to know them all.

Aid can be given in Three Different Ways

The United Nations recommend rich countries should give 1% of their GDP in aid. In fact, very few developed countries meet the UN criteria. The UK gives around 0.4% of GDP.

1) **Bilateral Aid** is where a **government** (e.g. the UK) gives **direct financial support** to another **government** that needs help (e.g. Malawi).

2) **Multilateral Aid** is from **international bodies** such as UNESCO, the World Health Organisation, the International Monetary Fund (IMF) and the World Bank. Multilateral aid can be either **grants** or **loans**. The IMF and World Bank give **loans**, and charge **interest** on the loans.

3) **Non-Governmental Organisations** (NGOs) give logistical support and direct financial donations. They get their money from the **public**. Examples of NGOs are Oxfam and Christian Aid.

Different Theories have Different Views of Aid

Modernisation theory says aid helps LEDCs "Westernise"

1) **Modernisation theory** believes that developed countries should give **aid** to countries that are prepared to accept Western styles of development, i.e. **industrial capitalism**.

2) Modernisation sees aid as having a **"trickle down effect"**. The argument is that aid goes to the elites of LEDCs, and the elite create wealth and prosperity. Associated factors such as **employment** and **increased standards of living** should **filter down** to **local economies** and **local people**.

3) Modernisation theorists were largely justified in the mid 20th century, as many poor countries (newly independent from colonialism) received aid and experienced **growth** and **success**. However, growth stalled later, and the poverty gap increased rather than decreased in some countries.

Neo-Marxist dependency theorists see aid as a tool to serve capitalism

1) Aid is often **tied** (given with conditions attached). A common condition is that local markets should be opened up to **free trade**, allowing foreign companies (including TNCs) to import and export goods without trade or customs levies. Neo-Marxists view this very **negatively**, believing that LEDCs are often exploited economically by TNCs.

2) **Bilateral aid** often requires the **recipient** nation to **buy goods** from the **donor** nation, or employ **technical experts** from the donor nation. These requirements help the **donor** nation.

3) Critics of Western aid such as **Teresa Hayter (1971, 1981, 1989)** see it as a tool for the richest countries to **politically influence** LEDCs. **Western** countries tended to give aid to countries with **right wing** governments rather than to countries with **socialist** or **communist** governments. This happened a lot during the Cold War.

4) To get a loan from the World Bank or IMF, LEDCs have often had to agree to make **political** and **economic changes** called **"Structural Adjustment Programmes"**. These are often **industrial-capitalist** in nature (e.g. privatisation of state run services). Evidence shows that some of these programmes **haven't succeeded** in developing poor nations.

New Right theory says that aid creates dependency

1) **New Right theorists** generally don't believe in giving anyone "something for nothing". They argue that aid teaches LEDCs to be **dependent** on MEDCs, rather than standing on their own two feet. They say that LEDCs start to see aid as a right, rather than as a safety net, or last resort.

2) **Neo-liberals** believe that aid mucks about with the proper operation of the **free market** — they think that the free market is the best way of encouraging development, through **enterprise** and **investment**.

International Trade and TNCs can help Development

A recent view is that **trade** is more productive in development strategies than **aid**. This view is influenced by the New Right.

Not all trade-based strategies are New Right theorists, though — e.g. the **fair trade movement** aims to **insulate** agricultural workers in developing countries from the **ups and downs** of the world market. Fair trade businesses pay farmers a fixed **"fair"** price for their crops, whatever the global market price is. Neo-liberals claim that fair trade is just **aid under another name**, and say that **subsidies** don't encourage producers to be efficient and enterprising. They'd rather leave it to the free market.

1) TNCs can have both **positive** and **negative** impacts on development in LEDCs and NICs. They **provide investment** to developing countries, which can help with their own national strategy for development. They also provide **jobs**, which increases the host nation's **wealth**. Workers in the host nation have increased **spending power**.

2) TNCs can cause **rapid economic growth** which can be **too fast** for a host nation's **infrastructure** to cope with.

3) Those who define development in quality of life terms are concerned about **working conditions** in TNC factories.

Strategies for Development

NGOs and Charities mainly provide Emergency Aid

1) **NGOs** and **charities** such as Oxfam, Save the Children and the Red Cross/Red Crescent mainly respond to **emergencies** — e.g. the 1984 **famine** in Ethiopia, the crisis in the Darfur region of Sudan and the 2004 **tsunami** in South East Asia.

2) **Disaster and emergency relief** is obviously a **short-term** thing. It's different from **long-term development strategies**. That being said, economic and social development **can't take place** where large numbers of people are starving or homeless. It's essential to **fix** the **immediate damage** before going on to **plan strategies** for the long term.

3) NGOs also participate in **development**. They develop **local communities** through education and village clinics and work with **governments** and **businesses** to co-ordinate national development.

Four stages of NGO and charity involvement

1) Relief and aid	Food programmes, urgent medical care
2) Community Development	Community health centres, community education
3) Systems Development	Working with government and private business
4) People's Movements	Encouraging locally managed development

Many LEDCs face a Debt Crisis — they spend more on Debt than Investment

Throughout the 20th century, **LEDCs** have had to **borrow money** from **richer nations** and **international organisations** both for survival and for development. The **World Bank** and **International Monetary Fund (IMF)** have lent large sums of money to LEDCs to fund development projects.

The World Bank and IMF are clubs which loan money to fund development projects in member countries. It's not just LEDCs who borrow money — the UK has taken out loans from both organisations.

1) If you ask for a **loan** from your **local bank**, it'll come with a set of conditions — you have to pay **interest**, you have to pay a certain amount **back** each month, and if you **don't** pay it back they'll take your house off you. If you don't pay enough off each month, the **interest** starts to **pile on**, and you can find yourself in **financial trouble**.

2) It's exactly the same with **nations**. Many poor countries spend **more** repaying **debts** and the interest that's built up on their debts than they spend on their own **infrastructures**. As **Hayter** points out, that's **not good** for **development**.

Dependency theory puts the crisis down to colonialism, corruption and greed.

1) Dependency theorists argue that many countries are poor because **colonialism** restricted their economic development. Countries that gained independence were forced to **borrow money** to invest in development.

2) Dependency theorists also argue that aid doesn't go to the right place — much of the aid given to countries is absorbed by **governments** who either **embezzle** the money (i.e. steal it for themselves) or invest in products that **don't help** a country to develop (e.g. **weapons**). There's an **investment gap** that has to be filled with **loans**.

3) In the 1980s and early 1990s, the **richest nations** and the **international lending organisations** significantly raised levels of **interest** paid on loans. Countries had to **borrow more** to meet **interest payments**. Dependency theorists think this rather suited the West as they saw an **increase** in the **debt owed** to them — they were suddenly looking at receiving a lot **more money** in debt repayments from the poorer nations.

There's an ongoing **campaign** to **reduce debt**, or **scrap** debts entirely. Many countries have had their **total debt** reduced, but this hasn't **yet** made a significant impact on the absolute poverty experienced by people within the poorest nations.

Practice Questions

Q1   What are the three types of aid that can be given to less developed countries?

Q2   Explain how the "trickle down effect" works, according to Modernisation theory.

Q3   What are the causes of debt according to dependency theorists?

Exam Question

Q1   "Aid is merely a tool for spreading capitalism across less developed countries". Assess sociological views on this statement.

(40 marks)

Lend us twenty million euros, would you...

You've probably heard Bono banging on about debt in developing countries, unless you've been in a cave on the moon with cushions strapped to your ears. You might even have heard him there — being a rock star, his voice does carry a fair way. You probably haven't heard of all the theories and sociologists' names on these pages, though, so you'll need to learn them for later.

Urbanisation and the Environment

Some sociologists say that cities are a focus point for modernisation, investment and economic development. Others say that development in cities doesn't help the poor, and damages the environment too much. The rest just live in them and leave it at that. Those last ones are my favourite type of sociologist. There don't seem to be enough of them.

Urbanisation goes along with *Industrialisation*

Urbanisation means the increase in **urban populations**, compared to **rural populations**. During periods of industrialisation, people have **migrated** from rural areas to urban areas in search of **work**.

Industrialisation means the change from **agriculture** and small scale "cottage industry" to large scale manufacturing in factories. Factories are **centralised workplaces** — they require people to move to where the work is.

In Western Europe, there was a **rapid increase** in urban populations in the **19th century** as a result of **job opportunities** offered by the **Industrial Revolution**. In Mexico, industrialisation and urbanisation happened in the **20th century**.

Modernisation theory argues that *Urbanisation* is key to *Development*

1) In **modernisation** theory, the growth of cities symbolises the triumph of Western models of development and Western ideals. The city is seen as a place that rejects traditional goals and aspirations and replaces them with notions of **meritocracy**, **activism** and **individualism**.

2) **Hoselitz (1964)** argues that the **cities** encourage people to **work**, and contribute to the economy, because the system within **urban** areas is focused on **achieved status** (success based on achievement rather than social position) and **meritocracy** (allocation of people to positions in society based on **ability** rather than **family**).

3) Critics of this theory argue that it is **ethnocentric**, because it's based on Western cities, Western capitalism and Western ideals.

4) Additionally, it's seen as rather **unclear** in places — it doesn't say how power, wealth and development move from urban areas into rural areas, it just **assumes** that they do.

Ethnocentrism refers to an idea that one set of cultural values are <u>superior</u> to another. It's normally used in the context of the West versus other cultures — to say a theory is <u>ethnocentric</u> usually means it sees everything from a <u>Western point of view</u>.

Some see *Development* as the move from *Rural Lifestyles* to *Urban* ones

1) Some sociologists, especially modernisation theorists, see development as the shift from the characteristics of **rural** life to **urban** life.

2) Taking this view means that it's **easy** to measure development — it's just a calculation of how **urbanised** society has become. This can be measured by counting the number of **cities** and urban townships, and the numbers of **people living, working** and **socialising** within them, and comparing it to the number of people who live, work and socialise in the countryside .

Dual Economy theory says that *Rural* and *Urban* economies are *Separate*

1) **Dual economy** theorists argue that urbanisation leads to two very **different** types of society within one country — **rural** society and **urban** society. They function as **two separate economies** with little connection between them.

2) The **rural** economy is **localised** and focused on **subsistence**. The **urban** economy is **national** and **international** and focused on **economic growth** and development.

3) The theory is based on the idea that **colonialism** pushed progression in **urban** areas at the expense of **rural** areas, which became marginalised.

See p.24 for more on colonialism.

4) It's a useful theory to explain the point that the needs and problems of **urban** areas are very **different** to **rural** areas.

5) However, **critics** point to the fact that dual economy theory still assumes that rural economies are "**backward**".

Dependency Theory — *Poverty* in LEDC cities is caused by *Colonialism*

1) **Dependency** theorists believe the cities described by modernisation theorists don't exist. They say cities in LEDCs aren't success stories of meritocracy and achieved status, where hard work always brings big rewards. They're actually polarised between the "**haves**" and the "**have nots**". They blame **colonialism** for this.

2) Dependency theory says that urbanisation **doesn't** bring solutions to the developing world, just more **problems**, e.g. inequality, urban poverty, bad public health. The developing world doesn't have the **infrastructure** to deal with these problems — there's poor health care, limited access to education, and little social security (if any at all).

3) According to the theory, only the parts of the city where **capitalist elites** live and work are anything like the modernisation theory model of a city. Those parts were **designed** under colonialism to house the **colonial elite**.

4) The theory says LEDC cities depend on trade with rich nations, and serve rich nations rather than their own people.

5) Dependency theory **ignores** countries where urbanisation actually **has** brought **economic benefits** for the people.

Urbanisation and the Environment

Development and industrialisation always has an Impact on the Environment

1) Industrialisation **creates** air, water and land **pollution**, and **uses up natural resources**.
2) Rapid urbanisation results in **overcrowding**. Urban **infrastructures** often **can't cope** with the influx of people. Rural-urban migrants settle in makeshift **squatter** settlements without a proper **water supply** or **sanitation**.
3) Urban areas are polluted by **industry** and by **motor traffic**. This affects **public health**.
4) The new **international division of labour** means that polluting heavy industry is concentrated in LEDCs.
5) LEDCs don't have **equal access** to "clean" technology — e.g. equipment to reduce air pollution from power plants.

There are different Theoretical views on how to Manage the Environment

The Neo-liberal view — there's a trade-off between pollution and economic development

1) Countries need to calculate the **costs** and **benefits** of any development strategy. Economic development usually has environmental costs such as deforestation, drought and loss of productive land space.
2) If a country works out that this cost is too high compared to the benefits of a development strategy, then they won't pursue that strategy. This may have an impact on their **competitiveness** in the **international economy** — they'll be less economically competitive compared to countries that have decided to go ahead with the strategy.

The Structuralist view — the debt crisis needs to be solved first.

1) The desire by developing countries to share in the benefits of capitalism results in countries always favouring **economic** development over **environmental** concerns.
2) **Structuralist** theories make the assumption that the developing world would ◄── be able to do more about environmental issues if it were free from debt.

> **Structuralist** theories are ones which say the <u>structure of society</u> is responsible for social problems. <u>Marxism</u> is a structuralist theory.

Some sociologists argue that Sustainable Development is the solution

1) **Sustainable development** has been high on the development agenda over the last 20 years. It's a strategy that looks for **solutions** to development problems that don't have **negative consequences** on the environment.
2) Neo-Marxist **Redclift (1987)** points out that the idea of sustainable development is **only needed** because development is defined in **economic** terms and characterised by trading **natural resources** for **money**.
3) Redclift also says that some environmentalists who **claim** to be in favour of sustainable development don't give high enough priority to the needs of the **poor**. Redclift says sustainability must be about **policies** to **manage resources** in such a way that they continue to meet the **basic needs** of the **majority** of people — i.e. it requires **political effort**.

There are Conflicts between the Green Agenda and Brown Agenda

1) The **Green Agenda** is a global initiative to reduce the impact of human activity on the world's ecosystems.
2) The **Brown Agenda** is an initiative of the **World Bank** to improve **environmental health** in LEDC cities.
3) The Green agenda is about **long-term** impact on a **global** scale, while the Brown Agenda is about **short-term local** action. Action taken to fix urban environments on the Brown Agenda may go **against** the Green Agenda.

Practice Questions

Q1 What is urbanisation?
Q2 What is the dual economy theory?
Q3 What do neo-liberals say about the conflict between environment and development?
Q4 What is sustainable development?

Exam Questions

Q1 Assess the ways sociologists have explained the relationship between urbanisation and development. (40 marks)

Q2 Critically evaluate the argument that concerns for economic development must come before environmental issues. (40 marks)

Pop another environmentally friendly non-wood log on the fire...

When you look at interpretations of urbanisation, remember that modernisation theory and dependency theory are pretty much opposite. So, given that modernisation theory says that cities are wonderful and promote development, dependency theory must say they're awful. If modernisation theory says something is black, dependency theory says it's white. And so on.

Aspects of Development: Education

You might not be in the mood to believe this, but good education has been proven to improve standards of living, raise participation in civic activities and make for a happier, harder working populace. In the last fifty years, developing countries have spent more of their budgets on improving the education of their people — with mixed results.

Good Education *improves the* Living Standards *of people in LEDCs*

Education is necessary for **development**. In Rostow's model of development (see p.22), an educated workforce is necessary for industrial take-off. Many other sociologists think education is very important for development.

1) **Economic development** requires expert, technical knowledge on a local level. Not all expertise can be brought in from other countries. International organisations and MEDCs are generally keen to see LEDCs **train** their own people in the **specialist skills** required in the long term development of a country.

2) Education also gives people the **values** and **attitudes** required in the process of development. Literate, numerate people can fully understand what action is required for development and **participate** in deciding what action to take in their communities and their country.

3) Education can act as a **unifying force**. It can give people a common set of **values** and ideas about their country, which helps to overcome class, ethnic and religious **differences** in a country.

4) Many people in the developing world are keen to participate in education because they want to obtain **achieved status** — a qualification, improved employment opportunities, etc. Education acts as an **empowering** tool for groups in society that have traditionally been **excluded** from **social mobility**, e.g. women and the poor.

Universal Education *is still* Unavailable *for many in the* Developing World

1) **External aid** and increased **investment** in the developing world has led many countries to introduce **universal education** — but provision is often **patchy**.

2) Some countries have universal education for **primary school** age (up to about 11 years old), some have universal education up to 14 or 16 years old, and some still haven't introduced universal education.

3) Even in countries that have **universal education** as a policy, not every child **actually goes to school**. This is because of other **family commitments** and needs — e.g. children may be required to **work** on the **family farm**.

4) In many countries, parents still have to **pay school fees** to get their child into school. Also, **school supplies** aren't provided by the state like they are in the UK. Families have to **buy** books, pens, pencils, erasers, school uniform etc.

The Growth *in* Education *doesn't mean* Quality Education

Much of the **increase** in education has had to be supplied by education **systems** that were designed to meet the **basic needs** of a **few**. Basic education systems have been put under **strain**.

Lessons aren't always of **high quality**. Some education doesn't provide enough **useful knowledge**.

The Growth *in* Education *has raised problems with* Employment

1) While young people are in schools and colleges being educated, they're not out **working** and contributing to the **local** and **national economy**.

2) Because more people are studying and fewer people are working, governments get less revenue from income tax. Governments have less money coming in but have to **pay out more** to **provide education**.

3) Bright, educated people from rural areas tend to **migrate** to the **cities** to look for jobs. This contributes to **over-urbanisation** and urban **overcrowding**.

4) The more educated citizens **sometimes struggle** to find **employment** in their own country, or they can simply earn a lot more by moving away to countries that have **better job prospects** — this is called the "**brain drain**", by the way. The end result is that the country **fails to develop** because the educated have **left**, to use their education elsewhere.

Marxist Dependency Theorists *see* Education *as* Cultural Imperialism

Dependency theorists really frown on the idea that education **trains** people for **development**. They **strongly disapprove** of education that gives people the **values** and **attitudes** that are needed for "imperial-capitalist" (i.e. Western) development — they call this **cultural imperialism**.

Dependency theory sees **education** as a potential **tool** for keeping people **culturally** and **economically dependent** on the developed world — it trains them to get the kind of **jobs** that **benefit TNCs** and the **developed world**.

Aspects of Development: Health

At the start of the 21st century, health in the developing world is still poor compared to the developed world.

Physical Quality of Life Index (PQLI) Measures Health and Education

1) **David Morris** developed the PQLI in **1979**. It measures **infant mortality**, **literacy** and **life expectancy**. It's useful for sociologists concerned with development as a social issue rather than an economic issue.

2) The PQLI also allows you to compare trends across countries. However, there are problems in collecting reliable data.

Education, Poverty and the role of MEDCs all impact on Health in LEDCs

1) Poverty forces people to suffer poor **public health** and a **bad diet**.

2) It also prevents them from gaining a good quality of **health care**. Universal free health care is **rare** in the developing world — people usually have to **pay** to see a doctor. There are also **not enough doctors** and **nurses** to go around.

3) The lack of good **health education** in the developing world means many people (particularly those in traditional, rural areas) do not know how to **prevent disease** and are not aware of **basic treatments**.

4) Drugs companies may sell drugs in the developing world that **can't be sold in the West** because of **safety** reasons. Or they may set the **price** of life-saving drugs so **high** that many in LEDCs can't afford them.

5) **Western products** may be used **inappropriately**. For example, **baby formula milk** is heavily advertised in LEDCs. Some mothers don't have access to **clean water** to make the milk with, so many babies die from **infections**. Also, poor mothers may **water down** the formula too much (to make it last longer), resulting in **malnutrition**.

6) Also, TNCs that have set up in the developing countries often pay little attention to the environment, or health and safety. For example, the Bhopal poison gas leak of 1984 happened because safety procedures were inadequate.

> **Example: HIV/AIDS in South Africa**
> - **Insufficient health education** in poor areas meant people **didn't know** how HIV was transmitted.
> - Clinics could be a **day's walk** away.
> - **Transnational drugs companies** refused to allow local drugs companies to make **cheap versions** of anti-HIV drugs. This was overturned by the courts in 2001.
> - In the 1990s, the **South African government** was **reluctant** to **distribute** anti-HIV drugs. *They doubted that HIV caused AIDS.*

There are different Theoretical Views about Health Inequalities

Modernisation theorists believe **Western** medicine is **superior**, and that Western medicine and **health education** would **solve** the problems of **high infant mortality** and **low life expectancy**. **Rostow (1971)** said that **high tech medicine** used in the developed world should be **transferred** to developing nations so that **quality health care** can be provided.

Marxist **Navarro (1976)** believed that high tech Western health care is not the immediate priority for the developing world. Poor nations need to focus on **basic health procedures** to **save lives** and **improve quality of life**. Doctors from these nations need to be encouraged to stay and work in their own countries, not to migrate to MEDCs for better pay.

Dependency theory blames **colonialism** and **exploitation**. Colonialism introduced European diseases to Africa, America and Asia. Colonialism also replaced food crops with cash crops, resulting in malnutrition. Dependency theory also blames the developed world for **poverty** and **debt**.

Practice Questions

Q1   What are the advantages and disadvantages of universal education?

Q2   What is PQLI?

Q3   What do modernisation theorists argue is crucial for development in health?

Exam Questions

Q1   How can education be used as a tool for development in the developing world?   (12 marks)

Q2   Critically evaluate the argument that the health concerns of the developing world have largely been caused by the policies of the developed world.   (40 marks)

This subject is certainly draining my brain...

With every page it feels emptier and emptier, and soon there will be nothing left. Anyway, it's those dreaded words "cultural imperialism" again. It's really hard to think about development without slipping into some kind of "them and us" thinking — either assuming that the West knows best, or assuming that the West is all bad, and that poor countries should be left to get on with it.

Aspects of Development: Gender

Recently, sociologists (particularly feminists) have pointed out that women and men experience development and under-development in different ways. And you know what that means — more radical feminists. Should be interesting.

There's **Gender Inequality** in the **Developing World**

Evidence from studies into gender in the developing world shows that in many cases women get a worse deal than men.

- Women have **lower life expectancy** than men in **some countries** (usually women live longer than men).
- Women are **paid less** than men.
- Women get **less education** than men.
- Women's **health** is **poorer** than men's health, and women have **less access** to health care than men do.
- There's even a greater chance a woman will have an **abortion** if a foetus is **female**.

The Gender Empowerment Measure (GEM) is a indicator of the progress made by women in a society

1) The GEM focuses on **social indicators** of gender equality — female and male participation in **decision making, economic participation**, and **economic power**.

2) In other words, it monitors whether women have the right to **vote**, how many women there are in **parliament**, how many women have **top management jobs**, and the **GDP per capita** of the **female population**.

3) This measure has continually shown that women haven't reached **social equality** with men.

The Gender-related Development Index (GDI) measures several development-related factors

1) The GDI measures **life expectancy, literacy**, years in **school**, number of **women in work** and **women's income**.

2) It has a more **positive** story to tell about women and development. Sure, men still generally have better income, literacy and so on, but women have **improved** in most categories for development.

3) **Women's literacy** and **numeracy** has improved, and the chances of death during or after **childbirth** has fallen.

Some say **Women** feel the **Negative Side Effects** of development **More** than **Men**

1) According to Marxist feminists, women experience a **dual burden** of **paid work** and **domestic responsibilities**.

2) When a country **industrialises**, men go from **one** form of work (agriculture) to **another** form of work (manufacturing industry), but women go from **one** form of work (housework and childcare) to **two** forms of work (housework and childcare plus a paid job outside the home).

3) Women in developing countries often work **longer hours** than **men**, in poor conditions.

This is quite simplified, and it's a broad generalisation anyway.

Technology can change **Women's Employment Patterns**

1) **Swasti Mitter (1995)** writes about the impact of **ICT** on **female** employment in **developing countries**. She says that computer technology can be really useful to women — it allows them to work from home and work **flexible hours**.

2) Many ICT jobs which have been outsourced to NICs from MEDCs go to women — e.g. call centre jobs, data entry, medical transcription services.

3) Mitter points out that many women in developing countries like India, Malaysia and Brazil now work in **ICT**, but they're concentrated towards the bottom end of the work ladder.

Radical Feminists argue that **Development Benefits Patriarchy**

1) Radical feminists see development as a tool to make women more dependent upon men.

2) Radical feminists say TNCs actively seek to employ women as they are cheaper, more efficient, and docile.

3) If women do experience **improvement** in their position in society, e.g. **greater life expectancy** through better **health care** or **increased income**, it's because the **patriarchy** of the developed **world** allow it for **productivity** reasons.

Radical feminism can be **criticised** for failing to see the **exploitation** experienced by **men**.

Socialist Feminists believe **Socialism** can bring **Equality** to poorer countries

1) Socialist feminists argue that socialism can bring about a society that **isn't gendered** — i.e. that treats men and women **equally**. They push for **socialist revolution** that totally **changes** the way people see "men's jobs" and "women's jobs", as well as moving ownership of the means of production from capitalists to workers.

2) Socialist feminist **Mies (1986)** argues that traditional Marxism and capitalism both **undervalue** the work women do.

Aspects of Development: Demography

Demography is the study of population change. It's been a big thing in World Sociology since, well, forever.

High Population Growth can be a Problem

Malthus (1798) thought that population growth could cause problems — a population could grow faster than its capacity to feed itself. He pointed out that limited resources would cause death which would balance the birth/death equation.

Neo-Malthusian **Ehrlich (1968)** believed that the "population explosion" was putting too much stress on the resources of the world, leading the developing world, in particular, to experience problems such as famine and malnutrition. He believed over-population was damaging development and the environment.

1) The work of Malthus and Ehrlich has been used by **modernisation theorists** who argue that over-population in the developing world is one of the biggest obstacles to development. Any economic surplus has to be spent on feeding the population and building an infrastructure to cope with increased population, instead of on industry.

2) In addition, modernisation theorists criticise the **anti-contraception policies** of **religions** such as Roman Catholicism for fuelling the over-population problem.

3) Modernisation theorists argue that the solution is to persuade governments to **promote birth control**, and for **Western governments** and **international organisations** to **fund birth control** programmes. Modernisation theorists also suggest that money should be spent on **educating women**, because educated women tend to have fewer babies.

Modernisation Theory's approach to Demographics is Criticised

1) **Modernisation theory** is criticised for blaming the **wrong people** — it puts the blame for over-population at the feet of the **governments** of the developing world, **religious organisations** and the **people themselves**. Marxists would blame the global capitalist system instead.

2) The theory is based on **statistical data** from the time of writing — the facts may have **changed** since the study was written. When Ehrlich was writing, the rate of population growth was increasing. Evidence from **Carnell (2000)** shows that the **prediction** made by Ehrlich is wrong — annual population growth has actually slowed.

3) **Harrison (1990)** points out that **birth rate** isn't the problem. Population growth is caused by a **decline** in the **death rate**, especially the infant mortality rate. People are having the same number of babies, but **fewer** are **dying**. Harrison does agree with Ehrlich that population growth threatens the environment, though.

4) There's actually not a lot of evidence that **food resources** aren't coping. **Food production** has **increased**, and the world has the capacity to produce **more** food than it produces now. **Boserup (1965)** said that **population increase** determined **agricultural change**, so that agricultural production always kept up with the population.

5) **Dependency theorists** argue that the West continues to take the very best resources a developing nation has, leaving the inhabitants with little land of any quality. **Land reform** and **redistribution** to the poor would be a better solution rather than population control.

The food supply looks fine to me...

6) **Adamson (1986)** believes that **poverty** causes **high population**, rather than vice versa. Poverty forces people to see children as **economic assets** who will bring money into the household and support them in **old age**. People often have large families as a means of economic survival. Parents can't guarantee that their children will survive into adulthood, so they have more children to increase the chances of at least one surviving into adulthood.

Practice Questions

Q1 What are the findings of the GEM and the GDI? Why do they differ?
Q2 Why do Modernists believe over-population is an obstacle to development?
Q3 Why do sociologists argue that over-population is understandable?

Exam Questions

Q1 What are the causes and consequences of over-population in the developing world? (12 marks)

Q2 Assess the argument that women are disadvantaged in the developing world. (40 marks)

Sometimes it's hard to be a woman...

... Givin' all your looove to just — one maaan. Oops, the radical feminists wouldn't be impressed with that at all. I bet it's actually quite hard being a radical feminist. Blaming men for everything that's wrong with the world must use up a lot of energy. And soon it's going to be hard being anyone at all because the world will be full up and there won't be any room to lie down.

Theory: Consensus Structuralism

*Structural perspectives analyse society as a whole system made up of different parts that mesh together. Structural approaches can be either consensus or conflict based. Consensus structuralism is pretty much the same thing as **Functionalism** (which you already know and love). It stresses the harmonious nature of society, something Durkheim called "social solidarity".*

Functionalists use the "Organic Analogy" to describe the Nature of Society

1) The **organic analogy** is used by **Talcott Parsons (1951)** to show how society acts like a **living organism**. An organism has a series of **organs** that are **interconnected** and **interdependent** with each other, and Parsons says that likewise **society** is a set of parts that are all **interconnected**, and all **interdependent** with each other.

2) Functionalists describe change as "**evolutionary**", which means that if there's a change in one part of society, other parts will **slowly evolve** to adapt to this change.

3) **Social ills** (such as excessive crime) have a **disabling** effect on certain parts of the organism (society), and they can gradually "infect" other parts.

> According to Functionalism, interrelations between the various parts of society can only happen because all members of society **agree** on **values** and **norms**. In other words, **society functions by value consensus**. These agreed values and norms are passed down from generation to generation through the process of "**socialisation**".

Functionalism says Society's Needs are met by Four Major Sub-Systems

1) **Functionalism** says all members of society have **needs** and **desires** that the **social system** must cater for. These needs can be broken down into **instrumental** needs and **expressive** needs.

2) **Instrumental needs** are **material** — e.g. the need to be fed, the need to have a home. These needs are supported by the **economic sub-system** (**industries**) and the **political sub-system** (**political parties** and **trade unions**).

3) **Expressive** needs are **emotional** — e.g. the need to **belong**. They're looked after by a **kinship sub-system** (marriage and family) and a **cultural sub-system** (which includes schools and churches).

Functionalism tries to Explain Everything

1) Functionalism, through the work of **Comte, Durkheim and Parsons**, was the first real attempt to create a theory to explain the operation of the **whole of society**. This kind of theory is called a **macro-theory** — i.e. a **large-scale theory** as opposed to a **micro-theory** or small-scale theory.

2) It's useful in showing how all the main institutions of society, such as the **education** system and the **family**, are **linked** to each other.

3) It helps to explain activities and actions that superficially seem **unusual** or strange. An example of this is Durkheim's study of suicide (1897). In this study, Durkheim argues that **social structure** and problems in the modern world cause people to commit suicide. In this case, what seems to be an **individual act** is actually part of a **wider social picture**.

There's plenty more about suicide on p.56-57. Go and read it — it's relevant to this section.

Functionalism is Criticised for Ignoring Conflict and Maintaining Inequality

1) Functionalism is criticised for its focus on **harmony** and **co-operation**. It fails to take into account the **differences** and conflicts between groups in society.

2) It tries to see a **positive purpose** in **all aspects of society** — even aspects which many people would view as harmful and negative. Durkheim claimed that if a **social phenomenon** didn't fulfil a **function**, it wouldn't **exist**.

3) Functionalism has been seen by critics as a **conservative** approach to society that **upholds inequality** and injustice. Critics say the problems suffered by the working classes, women and ethnic minorities have not been adequately explained and justified by Functionalism.

4) Functionalism has an almost **fatalistic** approach to the nature of **inequality** in society — it's seen as inevitable. Functionalists such as Parsons talk about "**meritocracy**" which is the idea that people succeed or fail based on their own merits. This suggests that society is **already fair**, so it's pointless to make things more equal.

5) According to Functionalists, **conflict** in society is **minimal** because people **accept** the **inevitability** of inequality. **Conflict theorists** (see p.35) definitely disagree on this.

Functionalism says that these hairstyles have a purpose in society.

Theory: Conflict Structuralism

Marxism is conflict structuralism. Marxists acknowledge that society is made up of institutions that work together. However, they believe that there is a conflict of interests between two different groups in society: the bourgeoisie and the proletariat.

Marxism says **Capitalist** society has created **Two Classes** with **Different Needs**

1) According to **Marx (1867)**, the ruling class own the means of production, and the working class work for the ruling classes without owning or controlling the means of production.

2) Marx explained change in society as the result of a **conflict of interests** between the **classes**.

3) According to Marx, the ruling class own the **infrastructure** (the means of production) and sustain their control over it by utilising the **superstructure** (the **institutions** within society e.g. religion, the education system).

4) In Marxist thought, the job of the superstructure is to legitimise the position of the ruling class through **ideological messages** within the institutions of society — i.e. society's institutions are set up to stop the working class gaining power, and also to make it seem OK for the ruling class to own and control everything.

5) Marx claimed that the proletariat (working class) are lulled into a **false consciousness**, which means they aren't fully aware of the **oppression** they suffer and how to **break free** from it. Marxists argue that only through **revolution** will the proletariat see how they have been oppressed, and then a socialist/communist society will emerge.

Neo-Marxism focuses on **Ideology** rather than **Economics**

1) Neo-Marxists such as **Althusser (1969)** and **Gramsci (1971)** have redefined the focus of Marxism by looking at the role of **ideology** rather than economic factors.

2) For example, Gramsci argues that the ruling classes can only maintain power through **gaining the consent** of the working classes by manipulative use of **ideology**. Althusser talks about **ideological state apparatuses** — e.g. the education system.

Marxism is criticised for its **Structural Focus** and **Determinism**

1) Marxism is **deterministic** — it assumes that oppression is inevitable for the working class, until a revolution happens.

2) Marxism fails to see everyday life in any other terms than "**class conflict**". **Ethnicity** and **gender** are largely **sidelined**.

3) Additionally, the fall of Communism in Eastern Europe has been used as evidence for flaws in Marxist theory. However many people argue that Eastern Europe didn't have **true Communism** anyway.

4) The increased affluence and consensual nature of many Western societies highlights the **lack of conflict**.

Weber was **Critical** of **Marxism**

Weber said that there could be **conflict** between **all kinds of groups** in society. He **rejected** **Marx's idea** that the division between **owners** and **workers** was the **only important division**.

Weber claimed that people were divided by **class**, **status** and **political** grouping. Weberian conflict theorists such as **Dahrendorf (1959)** argue that conflict is **much more complicated** than Marx had claimed. Dahrendorf argues that conflict is based on power and authority, not economics.

Practice Questions

Q1   What are the four sub-systems in society, according to Functionalists?

Q2   What is the main difference between Neo-Marxism and traditional Marxism?

Q3   What was Weber's main criticism of Marxism?

Exam Questions

Q1   Assess the influence of Marxist perspectives on sociological research.   (40 marks)

Q2   Compare and contrast Functionalist and Marxist theories on the nature of society.   (40 marks)

I'm barely functional before my first cup of tea...

You'll probably be at least a little bit familiar with these theories from other sections. It helps to have it all here, so that you can revise what you need to know for the Theory and Methods paper without getting it mixed up with other stuff. They can ask you about these theories, or about theories in general, so don't think it's something you only need to know for background.

Theory: Social Action

*Social action theorists focus on the interaction between individuals and small groups, rather than on the big structures of society. Social action theory is pretty much the same thing as **Interactionism** (which you already know and love...).*

Social Action sees individuals as "Social Actors" who Act rather than React

1) Social action theorists see people as **making their own choices**, and taking their own **action**, rather than being **controlled** by **social structure** or **reacting** to social structure. They see people's actions as key to studying society.

2) Social action theory is also known as **Interactionism** and **Interpretivism**. It claims that society is **constructed** from people's meanings, interpretations, behaviours and negotiations.

> The process of labelling is important for understanding how people interact on a daily basis. People observe the behaviour of others and classify that behaviour into various categories — e.g. responsible, or delinquent, or deviant. Social action theorists see labelling everywhere — in the family, in education, in health care, in the sociology of deviance, etc.

Social Action Theory sees Social Order as a Social Construction

1) Social action theorists argue that social order isn't something generated by **institutions**, either through consensus or conflict. Social order is **part of everyday life**, and they see everyday life as a series of **interpretations**.

2) They say social order is a social construction — a **product** of individuals' minds. They say people want to believe that there's order in society so they behave towards others in a way that **convinces** them that there **is** order. For example, they **follow social norms**, e.g. being **polite** to each other, **not stealing** from each other.

Social Action Theory rejects the idea that Sociology is Objective

1) The idea is that if you believe that people put their own meanings and labels on the world, you also have to accept that they can all put **different labels** and **meanings** on the **same action**. Every person will interpret an action (e.g. drinking alcohol regularly) slightly differently to others depending on the meaning they attach, e.g. one person might think it's a normal part of relaxing after work, and another person might think it's the first sign of alcoholism.

2) This means that sociologists **can't predict** people's behaviour as easily as structural approaches would suggest. People don't passively react to external stimuli in exactly the **same way** every single time. They act differently according to the **circumstances**, and according to their own **personal opinions**.

3) In other words, social action theory says sociology **isn't an objective science**. It's all very, very subjective.

Social Action Theory is Criticised for being so Subjective

1) Social action theory is **criticised** for its **subjective** and **relativist** nature. Critics worry that if the world is seen as subjective and based on assumptions and interpretations, then **nothing is true or false** — this would reduce sociology to a **mess of individual opinions**.

2) Structuralists argue that social action theory fails to properly address the **large scale structure** of society. They accuse social action theorists of concentrating too much on the **small scale**, and ignoring the **wider social context** that individuals act (or react) in.

3) Critics of social action theory also point out that social action theory doesn't really **explain social norms**. They're taken for granted as something we believe in, maybe because we want there to be some kind of social order.

This is a simplified version of Giddens' theory. The real thing is pretty abstract.

Structuration combines Structuralism and Social Action

1) Structuration theorists such as **Anthony Giddens (1984, 1987)** believe that there's a place for a strand of sociological theory and research that looks at both the **relationship between individuals** and their **social setting**.

2) Structuration theorists say that individuals are subject to **restrictions** and **pressures** generated by **social structures** and **social systems**, e.g. laws. But... they also argue that individuals **respond** to these in **different ways**. Individuals have an **awareness** of the social rules and structures and have **some level of choice** about how to react to them.

3) Structuration theorists say social structures are **open to change** — they can be **changed** by the actions of individuals.

Critics of structuration theory point out that institutions can **severely restrict** people's actions — not just affect them a little bit. Structuration theory assumes that if people want to change the world, they can manage it fairly easily. This is something that Marxists and feminists would disagree with.

Theory: Modernity and Postmodernity

Modernity refers to the Modern, Industrial, Ordered world

1) Modernity refers to the industrial world. It's linked to **urbanisation**.

2) It's also linked to the rise of **state bureaucracy**.

3) Modernity refers to a period of time when studies of the world were guided by **ordered**, **rational scientific** thinking. **Science** was seen as the answer, rather than the **traditional** sources of knowledge, such as religion.

4) Modernist sociological theories aim to **investigate** the world **scientifically**. They explain why societies have **evolved** to be the way they are, and explain why they're **arranged** in the way they are.

5) The Modernist theories are the **Structuralist** theories of **Marxism** and **Functionalism**. These are also called "**grand narratives**", which is a fancy way of saying "**big stories**", and "**metanarratives**", which is a fancy way of saying "stories that **make sense** of **other stories**". They're **big**, **all-encompassing stories** that explain **how** the world got to be how it is.

6) Modernist theories like Marxism claim a **monopoly of truth** — they claim that they're **objectively right** about the way the world is.

Postmodernism argues that Society has Progressed from Modernity

Postmodernists say that society today has **moved on** from the ordered industrial world of Modernity. They point to various **changes** in society:

1) **Work** has become more **flexible**, and service industries have partly taken over from manufacturing industries.

2) **Globalisation** has affected both **production** and **communication**. There's been globalisation of **consumption** and **culture**.

3) There's an emphasis on **consumption of cultural products**.

4) There's **pluralism of culture**, and **pluralism of roles**. People **interpret** society, and their own identities, in **different ways** according to the **circumstances** they're in (i.e. the same woman could have labels and roles of "mother", "wife", "friend" and "employer").

Postmodernists argue that sociology has moved into a time when "**metanarratives**" don't answer all the problems of the social world. Postmodernists say that there's a whole range of **competing theories** out there, which all have **something** to say about society. They argue that no one theory can claim a monopoly over the truth.

Postmodernism is Criticised by Structuralists and Social Action Theorists

1) Postmodernists emphasise the role of **culture** and the **media** in driving the creation of **identities**, **norms** and **values**. People no longer seek one answer to life but are happy to pick and choose values and identities.

2) This approach largely ignores the interactions between **individuals**, which **upsets social action theorists**. It also ignores the relationships between **social institutions**, which **upsets structuralists**.

3) Some sociologists **disagree** with the claim that we're living in a postmodern society. **Giddens (1990, 1991)** argues that we're actually in a state of "**high modernity**", with **high risk** of war, economic collapse or environmental disaster. He sees high modernity as like a **juggernaut** — a massive truck that's very powerful, and which could go out of control.

Practice Questions

Q1 Which is more important to social action theory — social structure or personal circumstance?

Q2 How does Structuration theory combine both structuralism and social action theory?

Q3 What is meant by the term "metanarrative"?

Exam Questions

Q1	Assess the influence of postmodernism on sociological study.	(40 marks)
Q2	Evaluate the usefulness of structural and social action theories in a study of society.	(40 marks)

When crossing the road, look both ways for the juggernaut of modernity...

Postmodernism is a lot easier to understand when you look at Modernism. Modernism has all these ideas about how the world should be, and how sociology should be, and Postmodernism decides to do the opposite. Remember that you can be asked about the usefulness of social theories in general to explain society, and that includes all the theories on these pages and on p.34-35.

Sociology as a Science

Some people wonder "Is Sociology a science?". Before you can answer that question, you have to ask, "What is science anyway?".

Science uses Experiments and Observation to Test Theories

1) Scientists collect data through **experiments**, **observation** and **measurement** in order to **test hypotheses** (a hypothesis is an unproved theory).

2) Science values **objectivity** (an unbiased viewpoint). Scientific statements are **based on evidence** which has been collected using **systematic**, **logical methods**.

There are Different Philosophies of Science

Obviously, it couldn't all be that simple. There are **different views** about **what science is all about**.

The Logical Positivist view of science is called the hypothetico-deductive approach

1) The researcher **observes** something, and decides it needs to be **explained**.

2) The researcher thinks up a **hypothesis** to **explain** the observed phenomenon.

3) The hypothesis is **tested** by **experiments**.

4) If the experiments **agree** with the hypothesis, then the hypothesis becomes a **scientific law**. Scientific laws are **universal** — they explain all phenomena which are similar to the one which was observed in the first place.

This process is called verification, which means checking that something is true.

Rudolf Carnap (1936, 1966) and Carl Hempel (1966) are examples of logical positivist philosophers.

Popper (1959, 1963) argued that experiments should try to prove the hypothesis wrong — this is called "falsification"

1) The idea is that you can't ever **prove** a hypothesis **100% correct**, no matter how much evidence you've got — but you can prove it **wrong** with just **one** piece of evidence that **contradicts** it.

2) For example, the hypothesis "all swans are white" isn't proved correct by seeing one flock of white swans. You'd have to look at **every single swan in the universe** and see that they were all white to do that. But if you see just **one black swan**, that proves that "all swans are white" **isn't true**.

3) Popper believed that it wasn't possible to know **absolute truth**, because you can't prove things are correct.

Popper's view has been **criticised** by later philosophers of science who point out that an experimental result that disagrees with a hypothesis may be because of **experimental error** and **silly mistakes**. In Chemistry practicals, you may not get the **predicted result**, but that doesn't mean you've **proved chemistry wrong** — it usually means you've made a **mistake**.

Thomas Kuhn (1962) disagreed with both the logical positivists and Popper

1) Kuhn believed that science uses an **accepted body of knowledge** to solve puzzles. He called this "normal science". He was pretty critical of it...

2) He thought that scientists took a lot of **assumptions** about the world **for granted**. This assumed **way of looking at the world** is called a **"paradigm"**. He said that what scientists do is **constrained** by the **paradigm** they take for granted. For example, for hundreds of years people thought that the sun went around the earth, and astronomical observations were interpreted according to the paradigm that the sun went around the earth.

3) Kuhn argues that **big leaps** of scientific progress come about when **evidence** which **doesn't fit the paradigm** builds up to the point where it **can't be ignored**. Then, scientists come up with a **new paradigm**. This process is called **scientific revolution**.

Paul Feyerabend (1975) went even further, and claimed that there **weren't** any **hard and fast rules** of scientific method. He argued that scientists make all kinds of **tweaks** to theories to make them work. He also disagreed with the idea that science tests hypotheses according to whether they fit observed facts, claiming that already-accepted theories **influence** the way scientists actually **observe** facts.

There's Disagreement about whether Sociology is Scientific

1) **Auguste Comte** (lived 1798-1857) invented the word "sociology", and he thought of it as a science. He thought sociology should be used to develop a **rational theory** of **society**.

2) **Popper** (see above) said sociology **wasn't a science**, and that sociological concepts **couldn't be falsified** by experiments.

3) **Kuhn** argues that sociology **doesn't have a paradigm** — there isn't a consensus as to what it's about and how it's done. So in his view, it doesn't count as a science.

Sociology as a Science

Sociology *is* More Subjective *than* Traditional Science

1) **Objective knowledge** is the **same** no matter what your **point of view**. **Objective** methods provide **facts** that can be easily **verified** or **falsified**. Objective research is also **value free** (see below), and doesn't have any bias.

2) **Subjective knowledge** depends on your **point of view**. **Subjective** methods give data that **can't** be easily tested. Subjective research requires **interpretation**.

3) Sociology is **more subjective** than the physical **sciences**, but it aims to be at least partly objective.

4) Some **postmodernists** like **Lyotard (1984)** claim that it's **impossible** to be objective at all. Lyotard sees **knowledge** as something that people **construct**, not something that people **discover**.

See p.36 for social action theory and subjectivity.

Positivist Sociology *tries to be as* Objective *as* Possible

1) **Positivists** think sociology should be **scientific** and **analyse social facts**. Positivists define social facts as things that can be **directly observed and measured**, e.g. the number of followers of Christianity in Britain. Positivists claim that social facts are **external** to individuals, and constrain their behaviour.

2) Positivists look for **correlation in data**, and **cause and effect relationships**. To do this, they use **quantitative** methods like **questionnaires** (see p.42) and **official statistics**, which are **objective** and **reliable**.

1) **Interactionist sociologists** (also called **interpretivists**) reckon **sociology doesn't suit scientific methods**. They try to understand human behaviour from the point of view of the **individual**, so they use methods that let them discover the **meanings**, **motives** and **reasons** behind **human behaviour** and **social interaction**.

2) **Weber** (see p.73) said it's important to use **empathy** to figure out **why** an individual is doing what they're doing. He called this **"verstehen"**. Interactionists take this idea very seriously — they're big on empathy.

There's Debate *over whether* Research *can be* Value Free

1) **Value free research** is research that doesn't make **value judgements** about whether the things it researches are **good** or **bad**.

2) Value free research doesn't let the **researcher's own beliefs** get in the way. For example, questionnaires mustn't ask questions that **lead** the respondent towards a particular answer.

3) In order for this idea of **value freedom** to work, the researcher must **interpret** all data **objectively**.

4) Value freedom means that the **end use** of the research **shouldn't matter**. Research should come up with knowledge, and how that knowledge is used isn't up to the researcher.

Some sociologists say **sociology can't be value free**.

1) The decision to research in the first place is **value-laden** — someone has to decide that the research is worth spending money on. Some say that research which the **state** or **businesses** want to see is most likely to get funding.

2) It's difficult to **completely avoid bias** and interview effects (see p.45).

3) Some Marxist and feminist sociologists **deliberately choose research** with an **end use** that they **approve** of. They believe that sociology **should** make **value judgements** about society and **suggest** ways it could be **better**.

Practice Questions

Q1 What is a hypothesis?
Q2 What did Popper mean by falsification?
Q3 What is a paradigm?
Q4 Why do some sociologists say sociology can't be value free?

Exam Question

Q1 Explain why some sociologists say that the study of sociology is scientific. (10 marks)

Don't even get them started on "What is Art?"...

*If you're flagging, remember that Sociology can lead to all sorts of **good jobs**. My mum did a Sociology degree and she's worked as a researcher, writer, lecturer, civil servant, NHS board-member and charity organiser. And if those kind of jobs don't tickle your fancy then there's also things like housing and social work. If you want to be a lion-tamer though, you're in the wrong book.*

Choice of Topic and Method

These pages are mainly revision of AS material — BUT there is some new stuff here, so don't skip over it.

Practical considerations Influence choice of Topic

1) Sociologists may **specialise** in a particular area where they have expertise.

2) **Funding** affects choice of topic. Government agencies often do research into areas covered by current or proposed **government policy**. **Industrial** grant providers tend to fund research that gives their industry some **practical benefit**.

3) Also, certain topics become popular in sociology at different times. For example, research in the **mid 20th century** focused on **stratification** and the **class system**. **Nowadays**, the focus of sociologists has moved on to other topics such as **World Sociology** and **Medical Sociology**. To gain **prestige**, **funding** and public or academic **interest**, sociologists are more likely to focus their research on topics that are currently **in vogue**.

Remember, data can be Primary or Secondary and Quantitative or Qualitative

- **Primary** data is gathered by the researcher, so it's **brand new** and **original**.
- It's as **valid** and **reliable** as the researcher's method makes it.
- It can be a **pain in the neck** to collect.

> Reliable data is data that someone else could get by using the exact same methods. Valid data is a true picture of what the researcher is trying to measure.

- **Secondary** data is gathered from existing data sets and documents.
- The researcher has to **trust** that it's valid and reliable — this is easier if they can find out the **original methodology**.
- It can **save time**, effort and money to use secondary data instead of primary data.

1) **Quantitative** research methods give **figures**. They're **highly reliable**. They may not be valid because quantitative data doesn't include anything subjective. Quantitative research can use **large sample sizes**, which makes it highly **representative** (see p.41).

2) **Qualitative** research methods produce **stories**, which include other people's **motivations** and **meanings** they give to what they do and think. They're **very valid**, but not very reliable. Qualitative research is **time consuming**, so it **can't use large samples**. This means it's **less representative** than quantitative research.

Theoretical considerations Influence choice of Method

1) **Structural** theories like **Functionalism** and **Marxism** favour **quantitative** methods.

2) **Functionalists** argue that the social world acts similarly to the **natural world** and therefore all study should be similar to that of "natural science" — i.e. using **objective** and **quantitative techniques**.

3) **Marxists** explain the nature of society in **economic** terms which also tend towards "scientific" techniques of data collection — i.e. quantitative methods.

4) **Social action** theories favour **qualitative** methods, because social action theory is **subjective**. For a social action approach, methods of data collection are more **small-scale** and **in-depth**. In order to analyse **why** people make the assumptions they make and act in the way they do, researchers **observe** and **question** them **at length**. Social action theorists prefer techniques that give detailed **stories** and **meanings** — e.g. ethnographic studies, unstructured interviews (see p.43) and observation (see p.44).

5) **Feminists** sometimes take a **falsificationist** approach. Feminist researchers may choose to look for evidence that proves a hypothesis **wrong** — e.g. evidence that gender roles **aren't** shaped by biological sex differences.

Practical considerations Influence choice of Method

1) Some methods take a lot of **time** — **qualitative** methods tend to **take longer** than quantitative methods.

2) **Funding** affects choice of method. The **researcher's time** costs money, **resources** such as computers cost money, and it costs money to send out **postal questionnaires** to large samples.

3) **Lack of access** to primary sources would mean that the researcher has to use **secondary** sources.

Ethical Considerations also affect choice of Topic and Method

1) **Consent** — all participants must have openly agreed to take part.

2) **Confidentiality** — the details of all participants and their actions must remain confidential and private.

3) **Avoidance** of **harm** — participants should not be physically or psychologically harmed by the research process.

4) **Avoidance** of **deception** — researchers should be open and honest about the study and its implications.

Research Design

Before you can Start — you Need a Sample

Population means the bunch of people you're surveying, not (usually) all 60 million people in the UK.

1) It's **too expensive** and **time consuming** for sociologists to involve all the people they want to study (the whole **population**) in their research. They select a **sample**.

2) When they select the sample they usually try to make it **represent the population** — with similar proportions of people in terms of age, class, ethnicity and gender to the proportions in the general population.

3) With a **representative** sample, the researcher can make **generalisations**. They can make statements about the **whole population** based on what they've found out about by researching the **sample**.

Probability Sampling involves Random Selection

Probability sampling involves picking names out of a "sampling frame" at **random**. A sampling frame is a **complete list** of the population being sampled, which needs to be **accurate**, **complete** and without any **duplicate** entries — easier said than done. **Random**, **systematic** and **stratified random** are all kinds of probability sampling.

1) In simple **random sampling**, names are taken completely at random, e.g. randomly selected from a list by a person or a computer, so each member of the population has an **equal chance** of being selected.

2) **Systematic** sampling involves choosing a **starting point** in the sampling frame and selecting every nth value, e.g. every fifth name. There may be bias, if there's an underlying pattern in the sampling frame.

3) In **stratified random sampling** the population is put into **segments** called "**strata**" based on things like age, gender or income — for example age 18-24, age 25-34, age 35-44, age 55-64, age 65+. Names are selected at random from within each segment.

Non-Probability Sampling involves Human Choice

Quota, multi-stage and non-representative are different types of non-probability sampling.

1) In **quota sampling**, the selection is made by the **interviewer**, who'll have a quota to meet — e.g. "interview 20 women between 25 and 34". It's a bit like stratified random sampling, but it's not random — interviewers tend to pick people who look "nice", which introduces bias. It's quick and useful, though.

2) **Multi-stage sampling** means selecting a sample from **within another sample**. It's often used to select samples for opinion polls to measure voting intention. First, a selection of constituencies are chosen to represent the whole country, then postcodes within that constituency are selected, then houses from those postcodes.

3) **Snowball sampling** means finding **initial contacts** and getting them to **give you more names** for your research.

4) Sociologists sometimes **deliberately** pick a sample who **aren't representative**, in order to try to **falsify** a hypothesis about social behaviour. For example, feminist sociologists trying to disprove the idea that gender roles are determined by biological difference deliberately looked for samples where women's roles **weren't different from mens' roles**, or weren't traditionally "feminine".

A Pilot Study is a Small-Scale Practice Run before the Real Research

1) A pilot study lets you **test** the **accuracy** of your **questions**, or **check** to see if there are any **technical problems** in your research design. Researchers do this to make the study **more valid** or **more reliable**.

2) You can also **test how long** the research will take and **train** your **interviewers**.

3) Pilot studies are **time consuming** and **expensive** and they create a **lot of work**. However, by showing that the project is feasible, they can help secure **research funding**.

Practice Questions

Q1   What does it mean to say that a study is: a) reliable, b) valid?

Q2   What is a sampling frame?

Q3   What is meant by each of the following — "systematic sampling", "quota sampling" and "snowball sampling"?

Exam Question

Q1   Identify and explain two methods of sampling that you could use for a postal questionnaire.   (4 marks)

What about the free sample...?

Sampling is a very important part of research design. It's one of the things that rival sociologists will really pick on if they think you've got it wrong. Remember that it's important to have a representative sample if you want to generalise from your results at all. The more random your sample, the easier it is to repeat your survey — good news for reliability.

Quantitative and Qualitative Methods

Although most of these methods were covered in the AS syllabus, they're on the A2 syllabus as well. The examiners need you to be more critical and evaluate the methods more at A2 than at AS though.

See the glossary or p.40 for a recap on the difference between quantitative and qualitative research.

Questionnaires *mainly provide* Quantitative Data

1) When planning a questionnaire, the researcher must first work out **how to measure the concepts** they're interested in. Some concepts in sociology, like 'norms' or 'anomie', can be **hard to measure**. To research concepts like this you need to transform the abstract idea into something you **can** measure, and this is known as **operationalising the concept**. You do this by finding **indicators** that are linked to your concept — e.g. for the **concept** of 'academic success', the **indicator** could be grades at GCSE.

2) **Closed questions** and standardised **multiple choice answers** give **quantitative** data.

3) You can do a questionnaire with **open ended questions** but it's harder to quantify the data into nice neat numbers. You could classify the answers into **categories** (this is called **coding**), but some answers might not fit.

4) Questionnaires should use **clear**, **simple questions** which are **easy to understand**.

5) They should give **clear instructions** and have a clear layout.

6) **Multiple choice** questions must give an appropriate number of responses. The researcher doesn't want too many respondents to answer "none of the above" or "other".

Questionnaires have several advantages

1) Questionnaires are **easy to administer**, and they can collect a **lot of data** in a **short time**. Closed questions provide quantitative data which can be **quickly** analysed too.

2) Questionnaires are **reliable**.

3) Questionnaires are **anonymous** and don't require the respondent to sit **face to face with an interviewer**. This makes them suitable for **sensitive topics**. For example, the National Survey of Sexual Attitudes and Lifestyles was a **postal questionnaire** rather than a face to face structured interview.

4) A **large sample** can be given a questionnaire, so they produce **representative data** that can be used to make generalisations.

Questionnaires have limitations — they aren't very valid

1) Respondents **may not tell the truth**. They may lie, or they may be mistaken.

2) Questions may be **misleading** or **mean different things** to **different people**. This means they may not accurately measure what you **want to measure**.

3) Respondents can't give any **extra information**, even if it would be really helpful to the researcher.

4) Because the respondent fills in the questionnaire on their own, there's no one there to **explain** the questions if the respondent doesn't understand them.

5) Postal questionnaires have a **low response rate**. If it's **too low** it won't be a **representative** sample.

Pilot studies (see p. 41) are useful for questionnaires. Researchers can test if the questions make sense to the respondents.

Structured Interviews *are* Questionnaires *given* Face to Face

1) Structured interviews are questionnaires given to individuals or groups, face to face.

2) The main plus point over a postal questionnaire is that the interviewer can **explain** and **clarify** the questions.

3) Also, most structured interviews get a much **higher response rate** than questionnaires. People tend to agree to be interviewed — unless the research topic is sensitive or taboo.

4) However, they're **more expensive** than questionnaires — you need to **pay for the interviewer**.

5) In a structured interview, the interviewer has to **follow the list of questions** so they **can't ask for more detail** if the respondent says something **particularly interesting**.

Social Surveys *use* Questionnaires *and* Interviews

1) **Social surveys** collect information about a **large population**, using **questionnaires** or **structured interviews**.

2) There are three main types — **factual**, **attitude** and **explanatory**. Some surveys are a mixture of more than one type.

Type of survey	What it's for	Who conducts it
Factual	Collects descriptive **information**	**Government agencies** and sociologists
Attitude	Collects **opinions**	**Opinion poll organisations** and sociologists
Explanatory	Looks for **reasons** and tests out hypotheses	Sociologists

Quantitative and Qualitative Methods

Unstructured Interviews give Qualitative Data

1) **Unstructured interviews** are **informal**, without a **rigid structure**. They use **open ended questions** and give **qualitative** data, so they're quite **valid**. Interviews are **flexible** — they can be used to find out facts or attitudes.

2) In a **fully unstructured** interview, the conversation just develops **naturally**. Interviews can be **slightly structured** and slightly **unstructured** — i.e. the interviewer has to follow the questions in a set order, but they can let the respondent **elaborate** on any interesting points, and they can **ask** the respondent for **more information.**

3) Interviews can be done with **individuals** or small **groups**. Group interviews let the researcher observe **interaction**.

4) Because they're used with **smaller samples than questionnaires**, they're **not as representative**. However, they're **more representative** than **participant observation**.

5) Unstructured interviews are good for researching **sensitive issues** where the interviewer has to gain the respondent's **trust** — for example sexuality, domestic violence, crime.

6) The interviewer needs to be **skilled** at their job and ask the **right questions** in order to find out the detail needed.

7) There are a lot of **interviewer effects** in an unstructured interview. The interviewee may say what they **think** the **researcher wants to hear**. There's more about interviewer effects on page 45.

8) It takes a **long time** to write up an **unstructured interview**. You have to write down a **whole conversation**, not just tick boxes for **multiple choice answers**. It's possible to do **limited categorising** of responses — the researcher could tick a box for a particular category of opinion expressed, for example the respondent saying "I'm worried about crime".

1) Interviewers usually use a **non-directive** style — they keep their own opinions to themselves, and they don't show any approval or disapproval of what the respondent says.

2) However, some sociologists choose to be more **aggressive** and **argumentative** in their questioning — more like a journalist. **Becker (1970)** took this approach when interviewing teachers, and claimed he'd got more useful information out of them than if he'd used the traditional non-confrontational approach.

3) **Ann Oakley (1981)** included unstructured interviews in her description of a "**feminist methodology**", and contrasted them with structured interviews, which she saw as masculine. She liked to get the respondent **involved** in the research process (known as **empowering the participant**), and sought to get more from them by becoming **close** to them.

Pilot studies allow the researcher to find out what kind of question gets a **substantial response**. They let the researcher find out whether they need to **warm up** with a gentle **chat** to gain **rapport** with the respondent before asking more meaty questions.

Longitudinal Surveys are done over a Long Period of Time

Longitudinal studies are done at **regular intervals** over a **long period of time**, with the same people. They're often **large scale quantitative** surveys. Some are more **qualitative** — e.g. the TV programme *Seven Up*.

1) You can **analyse changes** and **make comparisons** over time.

2) You can study how the **attitudes** of the sample **change** with time.

3) It's **hard** to recruit a **committed sample** who'll want to **stay** with the study.

4) You need **long-term funding** and you need to **keep the research team together**, which may be problematic.

Seven Up was a TV documentary that asked 14 kids aged 7 what they thought about life, and what they wanted to be when they grew up. The programme makers came back to interview them every seven years.

Practice Questions

Q1 Give two advantages and two disadvantages of questionnaires.

Q2 Give two advantages of unstructured interviews compared to questionnaires.

Q3 What is a longitudinal survey?

Exam Question

Q1 Examine the advantages and disadvantages of interviews as a method of data collection.   (10 marks)

Top tip: never subcontract your interviews to Trappist monks...

It's worth giving these methods a good going over, even if you think you remember them from the AS course. There's a little bit more detail here, and you're supposed to take a more critical approach at A2 level. That means you don't just learn what each method is, you have to be aware of pros and cons, and how to figure out if it might be appropriate for a particular topic.

Quantitative and Qualitative Methods

Sociologists can do experiments on people, or they can observe them — with or without the subjects knowing about it. Or, they can take the opposite approach and just read about people through secondary data.

Experiments provide Quantitative Data

- Lab experiments are done in a **controlled environment**, and analyse one variable in terms of another.
- They can be very **reliable**, but may not be **valid**, as it's hard to reproduce real social situations in a lab.
- They're mainly used by **psychologists**.

- Field experiments take place in **real social settings**.
- They're **valid**, but **less reliable** than lab experiments.
- They're mainly used by **interactionist** sociologists.
- Participants are more likely to be **unaware**.

Ethically, participants should give **informed consent**. However, some experiments **won't work** if the person studied knows the real purpose of the work. For example, if a person knows their obedience is being tested, they may be deliberately bolshy.

Observation provides Qualitative data about Behaviour in Real-Life Settings

1) In **covert observation**, the researcher **doesn't tell the group** they're being observed. The BSA advise that you should only use covert observation when there's **no other way** of obtaining the data.

2) **Overt observation** (direct observation) is when the group is aware of the research and they know who the researcher is.

3) **Participant observation** is when the researcher **actively involves themselves in the group**.

1) Participant observation gets the researcher **right to where the action is** — so they can **check out the dynamics of a group** from **close up**. The researcher gets **first hand insight** of people in **natural real life settings**.

2) **Participant observation** allows you to research the workings of deviant groups. **Humphreys (1970)** investigated men who secretly engaged in gay sex in public places (e.g. public toilets), by posing as someone who watched for a sexual thrill. These men wouldn't have wanted to take part in a study if Humphreys had approached them openly.

3) The researcher may get so involved that they can't **objectively observe** the group. A covert researcher **observing** a deviant group may be pressurised to join in with illegal acts.

4) Participant research is extremely **flexible**. The researcher can change their ideas based on what they see.

5) Participant research **lacks reliability** — it can't be repeated. A covert observer may find it difficult to **record** the study accurately, and without imposing their own subjective values on it. However, interactionists say observation can be used to assist more objective methods. **Becker (1970)** used observation to collect information that he used to formulate a **hypothesis**, which could then be checked out in further research.

6) There are **ethical** and **practical** problems in **getting in**, **staying in** and **getting out** of the group.

7) The research usually includes a **small group** so it's not **representative** of the population. **Goffman (1968)** studied just **one** mental asylum.

8) It's **hard work**, **time-consuming** and **expensive**.

Overt researchers may have a "sponsor" who gets them into the group. Covert researchers must pretend to be just like the group members.

4) **Non-participant observation** is when the researcher **observes** the group but isn't actively a part of the group.

5) **Ethnography** is the study of the way of life of a group, through observation, interviews, and diary keeping.

6) **Case studies** are detailed investigations of one thing — e.g. one person, one institution, or one event. Case studies **can** be used to falsify hypotheses. However, it's not possible to **generalise** from a case study — they **aren't representative**, because of their tiny sample size.

Statistics are a Secondary source of Quantitative data

1) **Hard statistics** are **objective**, e.g. statistics on births and marriages.

2) **Soft statistics** are more **subjective**. Statistics on **crime**, **poverty** and **unemployment** are soft statistics. In the 1980s and 1990s, the government **changed the method** used to **measure unemployment** over 20 times.

Secondary sources of Qualitative data include Documents and Mass Media

1) Documents can be **personal** (e.g. **letters**, **diaries**, **suicide notes) or official**, (e.g. **school records**, or **church** records)

2) Documents can be **expressive** — to do with **meanings**, like a **suicide note**. Documents can be **formal** — like **official letters**. **Interactionists** like **expressive** documents because they're a big source of **qualitative data**.

3) Documents can be **difficult to understand** if they're old. They might be **fakes**. Personal documents might contain **lies**.

4) The **mass media** is another source of **secondary data** about people and society.

5) Sociologists analyse **documents and the media** by looking at **content**, **themes** and **style of language** used. **Content analysis** can be **quantitative** or **qualitative**. **Quantitative** analysis **counts** the number of times a theme comes up in the text, or the number of times something happens. **Qualitative** analysis looks at the **meanings** of the text.

The Context of Data Collection

The way in which data is collected can seriously affect its validity.

Data must be **Valid** — the **Collection Process** can make it **Less Valid**

1) Respondents in an interview may **forget** things, **exaggerate**, or flat-out **lie**.

2) They may try to show themselves in the **best possible light**. They may say they **wouldn't commit crime** when **really they would**. They may say they **recycle all their rubbish** when **really they don't**.

3) **Criminals** interviewed by **Laurie Taylor (1984)** later claimed that they'd **made up lies** to see if Taylor **believed** them.

Asking people about their **attitudes** to an event a **long time afterwards** often isn't valid. People **change their views** over time, and may **alter their description** of the past in the light of their **current beliefs**. For example, a middle-aged person may **falsely claim** to have been law-abiding as a youth when really they were a teenage delinquent.

There's a danger in **participant observation**, particularly **covert** observation, that the researcher will "**go native**". This means they get **too involved** and find it **hard to stand back** and **observe** the group **objectively**. **Whyte (1955)** became so involved with the gang members he studied that he started to see himself as **one of them** — even though his research was **overt**.

Interviewer Effects can Alter the way Respondents Behave

Interviewer effects are also called "researcher effects".

1) Respondents in interviews may give the sort of answer they **think** the **interviewer** **wants to hear** — or the **exact opposite**, if they're feeling stubborn.

2) Interviewers can give **subtle direction** towards certain responses — often **without realising** they're doing it.

1) Participants in experiments may try harder at what they're doing to get a **positive response** from the researchers.

2) This is called the **Hawthorne Effect** — first observed in an experiment at the **Hawthorne** electricity plant in Chicago, analysed by **Elton Mayo (1933)** in his work on motivation. The experiment was **meant** to test worker responses to **changes in variables** such as **workplace lighting**, but in fact **productivity increased** with **each variable change**, positive or negative. The workers seemed to be responding to the fact that they **knew an experiment was going on**.

3) These effects mean data from experiments may not be **valid**.

The presence of a researcher affects the **behaviour** of the participants **being observed**. Also, the observation must be **interpreted** by the researcher, and the researcher's interpretation may be **biased**.

Cultural Issues have an Impact on Validity

1) **Labov (1973)** found that **black American children** were much **more forthcoming** with a **black interviewer** than a **white** interviewer. He suggested that this could lead white researchers to think that the children had poor linguistic ability.

2) Ethnicity wasn't the only factor — the children were most forthcoming in an **informal setting**, where they could bring a **friend** with them.

3) Labov's explanation was that the children didn't speak up and show their abilities when they perceived the situation as alien, or **hostile**.

4) **Oakley (1981)** thought that **women** responded to a **friendly** interview style.

The **acceptability** of some sensitive issues **varies** between **social groups**. Some social groups may be less keen on **admitting embarrassing** or **socially undesirable** things, e.g. deviant behaviour, or mental health symptoms.

Practice Questions

Q1 Give two advantages and two disadvantages of participant observation.

Q2 What is the Hawthorne Effect?

Q3 Why did Labov suggest that children were more forthcoming in an informal setting, with a same-ethnicity interviewer?

Exam Question

Q1 Assess the usefulness of participant observation as a research method. (40 marks)

But what do they do if all the respondents decide to lie...

That covert participant observation stuff sounds a bit cloak-and-dagger to me, almost like being a spy. I don't think I'd be up to it myself — after a point you must get sick of pretending to be a gang member or a neo-Nazi or whatever and just feel like going home for a nice cuppa. And after all that trouble, you could find that interviewer effects ruin your results. What a life.

Impact of Sociological Research

Social policy focuses on social problems and how social institutions respond to them. Social policy analysts use sociological research to inform governments and other organisations, and influence their response to social problems.

Giddens claims the study of sociology gives Four Practical Benefits

Anthony Giddens (2001) believes that sociological research has four practical purposes:

1) An **understanding** of the world.
2) A heightened awareness of the needs of **individual groups**.
3) An assessment of "**what works**" — **evidence based policy**.
4) An increased **personal knowledge** of ourselves and others.

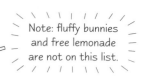
Note: fluffy bunnies and free lemonade are not on this list.

Sociological Research gives Policy Makers insight into Poverty and Inequality

1) The creation of the Welfare State after the second world war gave many the impression in the late 1960s that poverty had been largely eradicated from the UK.

2) However, **empirical evidence** from **Peter Townsend (1979)** and **Mack and Lansley (1985)** showed that poverty was a hidden problem. Later research by the Child Poverty Action Group reported that some groups experienced poverty more than others.

3) Sociologists then did more research to come up with theories of **why** certain groups were more vulnerable to poverty. **Social Democrats** blamed an **inadequate** welfare system, the **New Right** (e.g. **Marsland (1989)**) blamed **reliance** on an over-generous welfare system, and **Third Way** thinkers emphasised **citizenship** (two-way responsibility between the citizen and the state). (See the AS topic of Wealth, Poverty and Welfare).

4) These theories, plus **empirical data**, guided **social policy** about welfare, poverty and inequality.

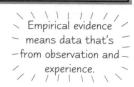
Empirical evidence means data that's from observation and experience.

This link between sociology and social policy was particularly close in the case of **Frank Field (1989, 1996)**, who wrote about the underclass as a group denied citizenship rights, and suggested **social policy changes** to improve the living standards of the elderly and unemployed, and to get the unemployed back into work. Between 1997 and 1998, as a **Minister** in the Labour government, he actually **was** a **social policy maker**.

Some believe Sociology should help Improve Society

Will Hutton (1995) argues that New Right theories have influenced social policy too much. He argues for a **Third Way** based on sociological research, and believes that social institutions should be made stronger, to provide better services.

Philanthropist **George Soros** believes in working towards **open society** — a society with the rule of law, democracy, and respect for minorities. He's influenced by **Karl Popper (1945)**, who first came up with the idea of open society.

Weber believed Sociology shouldn't tell decision-makers How To Fix Society

1) Weber believed that sociology **shouldn't make value judgements** — it shouldn't tell policy makers **how to fix society**.

2) Weber argued that sociological research can tell decision makers whether a particular policy is likely to have the **desired result**, and what **social costs** the policy will incur. Weber thought that the policy maker should come up with the **policy first**, and **then** the researchers should go away and find evidence to work out the best way of doing it.

3) Weber thought it was important to have **good methodology** to give the most **useful information** to policy makers.

4) Critics of this view say policy should come **after evidence gathering**, not before. There's a danger that only evidence which **backs up** the policy will be found. Evidence which might suggest a **much better policy** might be missed.

Postmodernists have Diverse Views on the link between research and policy

1) Postmodernist **Zygmunt Bauman (1990)** believes that sociology **should** inform social research, and worries that society may **get worse** if sociological theories about **poverty** and **welfare** aren't listened to. He argues that **postmodern consumer society** is **marginalising** the Welfare State, and believes this to be a bad thing.

2) On the other hand, Lyotard is worried that "**scientific**" methods of sociological research could be used to construct **oppressive metanarratives**. **Lyotard** sees **modernist metanarratives** (see p.37) as leading to **strict doctrine** and **oppression**. (Go back and read about metanarratives on p.37 if you're getting confused...).

Impact of Sociological Research

Marxists think sociology is Too Close to the Capitalist System

1) Marxists believe that sociology is too closely intertwined with the **capitalist system** to make a difference to society. Since Marxists believe that capitalism is inherently flawed and oppressive, they suggest that sociological study is a **tool** used to **justify unjust social policy**.

2) Marxists believe that research is **controlled** by **ruling class interests**, which prevents it from being used to change the system to socialism. They point to the amount of **funding** for sociological research which comes from the **state** and from **industry** — they claim sociology is being **bought**.

3) An example would be the use of empirical data to show that the poorest in society are over-represented in prison. Marxist commentators argue that sociology is being used here to **justify social policy** designed to **further oppress** and **marginalise** the working classes by focusing on crimes committed by the poor rather than looking at the underlying reasons for crime (i.e. the nature of capitalism, according to Marxist theory).

Some Feminists believe Sociology Can't affect Gender Inequality

Feminists are in **disagreement** over whether or not sociological research can actually improve the lives of women in a patriarchal society.

1) **Liberal feminists** believe that sociological research and analysis has influenced governments and had **beneficial results** for women's lives. For example, the UK has developed social policy designed to improve the status of women and make them equal in all spheres of social life including employment and benefits.

2) However, **radical feminists** argue that liberal feminist sociology can't **make much difference** to the lives of women because society is **inherently patriarchal**. Radical feminists such as **Shulamith Firestone (1971)** believe that patriarchal society must be dismantled before women's lives can ever be improved.

3) Socialist feminists claim that social policy oppresses women in particular. They argue it **undervalues women's labour** (e.g. in the voluntary and informal welfare sectors) and assumes they will bear a double burden of work and housework. Socialist feminists propose changes to social policy based on their own research and ideology.

"I 'ad that Tony Giddens round the other day to sort out me social policy. 'E were bloomin' useless."

Some believe the Link between Sociology and Social Policy isn't all that strong

Governments take account of research, but they're **constrained** by **other factors**.

1) Firstly, governments often seek to implement social policy that's **popular** with the **electorate**. It's argued that policies which aren't clear vote winners don't get implemented.

2) Some groups in society may be marginalised because they **don't vote** in **large numbers**. Even if sociology focuses on these groups, they may still find themselves neglected if they don't have electoral power.

3) Governments must consider the **financial implications** of any policies they introduce. If a policy is **too expensive**, then no matter how persuasive the sociological research behind it is, it **isn't going to happen**. Also, **expensive policies** tend to make **voters worry** that **taxes** might have to **increase** to pay for them.

Practice Questions

Q1 What four practical benefits does Sociology have for society, according to Giddens?

Q2 What role did Weber think Sociology should have in relation to social policy?

Q3 How do Marxists criticise the link between Sociology and social policy?

Q4 What other factors affect government decisions on social policy, other than Sociology?

Exam Question

Q1 "Sociology has no effect on social policy". How far do you agree or disagree with this statement? (40 marks)

Sociology, eh — what's it all for...?

In an exam, remember that all arguments in this topic are broken into three camps: 1) sociology should actively try and influence policy, 2) sociology should try to change and replace the system, and 3) sociology shouldn't influence social policy. Some people criticise sociologists such as Antony Giddens for overplaying the ability of sociology to influence government decisions.

Crime, Deviance and Social Control

For this whole section, you have to be able to relate crime and deviance to other areas of sociology from the AS course as well as the A2 course — e.g. health, the mass media, families etc. That means more revision for you, I'm afraid.

Here are some **Definitions** of **Crime** and **Deviance**

> **Deviance** = behaviour which goes against the **norms**, **values** and **expectations** of a **social group** or **society**.

> **Crime** = behaviour which **breaks laws** and is **punished** by the **legal system**.

Crime is deviant, but **not all deviance** is **criminal**. Think about it — it's hard to think of a criminal act which isn't also viewed as deviant but it's easy to make a long list of **non-criminal deviant behaviour** — picking your nose in public and eating it, cross-dressing, barking like a dog during a job interview, swearing at the referee, cheating at poker, etc.

Downes and Rock (1988) gave this definition of **deviance**: "Deviance may be considered as **banned** or **controlled** behaviour which is likely to attract **punishment** or **disapproval**."

Social Order and *Social Control* create a *Consensus* of how to behave

1) By definition, **most behaviour** in society isn't **criminal** or **deviant**. **Social control** is the way a society regulates the behaviour of its members and creates a **value consensus** of how to behave. People are **socialised** to follow social norms.

2) Some norms become **second nature**. For example — when having a **face-to-face conversation**, people manage to stand the right distance apart, look at each other when they're talking without staring excessively, be polite and tactful, not talk for too long — all **without really thinking** about it.

3) Other norms are followed because we're **consciously aware** that they're a norm — e.g. stopping at a red traffic light.

4) **Sanctions** are **rewards** and **punishments** that **reinforce** social norms. **Positive sanctions** are **rewards**, and **negative sanctions** are **punishments**. Sanctions can be **formal** (carried out by an official agency, e.g. giving a student a certificate for passing an exam, giving a driver a speeding fine) or **informal** (saying "well done", telling someone off).

Functionalists argue crime and deviance are *Useful* and *Necessary* in society

You might well wonder how on earth crime can be useful. Functionalists say it's because it has a **function** in society:

1) Crime and deviance can actually **help maintain social order** because it **unites** the **rest** of society in disapproval of the deviant behaviour. The majority **consensus** on acceptable behaviour is reinforced as people join together in outrage.

2) **Durkheim (1897)** said deviancy allows for **social change** to occur. Durkheim and the Functionalists who came after him argue that all societies need some change to remain healthy and stable. If society reacts positively to deviant behaviour it starts the process for that behaviour to be seen as non-deviant in the future.

3) **Durkheim** said crime moves from **functional** to **dysfunctional** when the level of crime is either **too high** or **too low**.
   - Too high, and it threatens social order.   • Too low, and there's no social change.

Albert Cohen (1966) identified two ways that deviance maintained *Social Order*

1) He argued forms of deviance such as **prostitution** provide a **safety valve** for releasing tension without threatening social stability.

2) Secondly, he argued deviant behaviour is used as a **warning device** by society to **identify** emerging **social problems**, which can then be dealt with, e.g. civil disobedience, protests, and truancy.

Merton said **Crime** *is a* **Response** *to* **Failing** *to* **Achieve** *society's cultural goals*

1) Functionalist **Robert Merton (1968)** concluded from his American study that the vast majority of individuals share the same goals but don't have equal access to the means of achieving these goals.

2) He identified the main cultural goal in American society as **success** and **wealth**. He said that the main (institutionalised) means of achieving that goal was through the education system. When individuals fail or are excluded from this system, this creates **anomie**. ← *Anomie = a lack of values, and feeling of purposelessness.*

3) Merton argues that individuals who fail at the standard route to success select **alternative** and **deviant** ways of reaching success and wealth — e.g. **crime**. These alternative paths are known as **modes of adaptation**.

4) Merton says they may also **retreat** from society — e.g. by **dropping out**, **drinking** to excess or taking **drugs**.

5) They may also **rebel** against society, and engage in **protest** and revolution to try and change society.

Crime, Deviance and Social Control

Subcultural theories say Cultural Values of some groups Encourage Deviance

Some deviance is **conformity** to norms and values – just **different** norms and values to **mainstream society**.

Cohen said delinquent gangs provide prestige for adolescents frustrated at their lack of status in society

Albert Cohen (1955) said that working class boys suffered from a lack of opportunities to succeed in mainstream society, largely due to cultural deprivation. This leads to dissatisfaction with their position in society — which Cohen called **status frustration**.

This tension is **released** by joining or creating groups which have **alternative values** to achieve status. These values tend to be the **reverse** of those of mainstream society — behaviour deviant in society becomes **normal** and **valued** in the subcultural group. For example, **petty crime** or **drug-taking** might be valued by the group.

1) **Cloward and Ohlin (1960) combined** the ideas of **Merton** with the ideas of **Cohen**. They believed there was a **legitimate opportunity structure** (passing exams and getting a job, as Merton said), and an **illegitimate opportunity structure** (being in a gang and committing crime, e.g. theft and vandalism).

2) They also argued that access to the **illegitimate** opportunity structure is **no more equal** than access to the **legitimate** system. In some areas, there are criminal gangs which provide adolescents a deviant route to success and status, and in some areas there aren't. This explained why **not all** frustrated working class boys turned to **crime**.

3) Cloward and Ohlin said that adolescents who have **failed** in **both** the legitimate opportunity structure and the illegitimate opportunity structure **retreat** from society and turn to drink or drugs.

Miller thought crime and delinquency come from Working Class Cultural Values

1) **W.B. Miller (1962)** said that general **lower working class culture**, not subcultural gangs, was what encouraged crime. According to Miller, working class subculture valued six main '**focal concerns**', including things like 'excitement' and 'toughness'. He claimed that criminal behaviour happened due to **obedience** to these norms of working class culture.

2) Miller was **criticised** right from the beginning. **Bordua (1962)** said that the idea that the working class live their lives **isolated** from the rest of society is **flawed to begin with**.

3) Miller's ideas have been supported by recent **New Right** sociologists. **Charles Murray (1990, 1993)** believes there's an underclass in British and American society with a **distinct culture** and **value system** which **encourages** deviance.

Matza said individuals Drift into Deviant Subcultures and Back Again

1) **Matza (1964)** argued that most delinquents **conform** to society's norms and values like everybody else for most of the time, but that under certain circumstances they can convince themselves that the law **doesn't apply** to them.

2) He thought that there was an **alternative** culture running **alongside mainstream culture** (or underneath it — he called the alternative culture "**subterranean values**"). According to Matza, this alternative culture values **spontaneity** and doesn't value responsibilities, so it provides a **break** from the usual commitments of life.

3) Matza argues individuals **drift** into this subculture at times of **stress** and **isolation** but most of the time remain outside of it, **conforming** to **mainstream** culture.

Practice Questions

Q1 What is meant by the following terms: "deviance", "social control" and "positive sanction"?

Q2 Why did Merton think people committed crime?

Q3 What is meant by "status frustration"?

Q4 What did Miller say was the cause of crime?

Exam Questions

Q1 Examine the ways in which the idea of social control can help in the study of one or more of the following: education; the family; work and leisure; mass media. (12 marks)

Q2 Assess the usefulness of Functionalism in explaining crime and deviance in society (40 marks)

Society made me do it...

Unlikely to stand up in a court of law, that one. I wouldn't recommend defending yourself by quoting Merton and Cohen. It didn't work for me after all that unpleasantness with the goat smuggling. Anyway, I'm not going into all that now. The past is the past. And I was actually doing society a favour — I was acting as a warning device that goats are not fairly distributed in the UK.

Crime, Deviance and Social Control

Deviance is controlled by society and kept to a low level. Some sociologists have a problem with the type of social control our society exerts, but at least it means you're less likely to be mugged by a naked nose-picker.

Marxists agree that Social Control keeps Order in Society

Marxist sociologists agree with Functionalists that social control is essential to keep order, but they **don't agree** that it **benefits everyone** in society. They say capitalism is an **exploitative** system which requires systems of social control over the population to **prevent rebellion and revolution**. Marxists say social control **benefits the ruling class** and works against the interests of the majority working class.

Marxists say social control is maintained through hegemony

1) **Informal social control** is achieved through socialisation, where individuals are **taught** to accept ideas and norms which support the status quo in society. These ideas are supported by **institutions** of the State such as the **education** and **legal** systems.

2) This ideology (set of ideas and values) is presented as **common sense** and neutral. However, according to neo-Marxists such as **Gramsci**, it's really designed in the interests of those in power.

3) Alternative ideas are overwhelmed by the **dominance** of this **ruling class ideology**.

4) The ability to **informally control** ideas and values in this way is **hegemony**.

5) Part of capitalist class hegemony is the **belief** that the legal system operates in the interests of **everyone** in society. Traditional Marxists argue the legal systems are actually methods of **formal social control** over the population. They claim the legal system backs up the ideas and values of the ruling class ideology.

Marxists say the Capitalist State passes Laws which benefit the Ruling Class

1) According to Marxism, laws **aren't the will of the people**. They're a reflection of ruling class interests.

2) Besides the most serious crimes of murder, rape and violence, the vast majority of law in the UK is **property law**. **Chambliss and Mankoff (1976)** wrote that most of this serves to keep **working class** people **away** from the property and land of the rich. The ruling class uses the law to protect **private property** because **capitalist exploitation** is built upon it.

3) The vast majority of the population have **no power** or **say** in the creation of **laws** and **punishments**.

4) The **lack of legislation** in some areas of life is also a demonstration of the law as an instrument of the ruling class.

5) Canadian sociologist **Laureen Snider (1993)** argues legislation regulating **large companies** is **restricted** in capitalist societies because it could **threaten ruling class interests**. For example, legislation regarding health and safety, pollution and fair trade are passed to a **minimum level** and often **weakly enforced**. **Tobacco companies** have put huge **pressure** on governments **not to pass laws** making them **legally responsible** for the deaths of smokers.

6) **Pearce (1976)** suggested that even the laws which supposedly protect the working class (e.g. health and safety laws, consumer laws) are really in ruling class interests. He said the system needs healthy, safe and loyal workers.

Marxists say Ruling Class law-breakers are Less Likely to be Punished

Marxists also say the laws which exist are not enforced equally in capitalist societies.

1) **Laureen Snider (1993)** argues that working class crimes such as burglary don't cause as much harm in society as corporate crimes such as breaking health and safety law.

2) Marxists suggest that **ruling class ideology** successfully presents the burglars as the "real criminals" and a threat to society, largely through the media. Meanwhile **corporate law breakers** get very little **media condemnation** and are treated more **leniently** by the legal system.

3) Also, if company bosses are charged they have the **money** to buy the **best legal advice**.

4) The work of **Chambliss (1978)** is good evidence for this. He studied crime in the American city of Seattle and found those in power were able to use it to conduct criminal activity and to avoid prison. He found an organised crime syndicate which included elite businessmen and politicians who used money and influence to bribe officials.

Gordon (1976) argues **selective enforcement** of the law and **selective reporting** in the media gives the impression that criminals are largely working class. He thinks this not only diverts attention from ruling class crime but also **divides the working class** when the working class criminal becomes the target of anger rather than the system itself.

Some Marxists see Crime as an Inevitable Consequence of Capitalism

Crime such as robbery and property theft is seen by traditional Marxists such as **Bonger (1916)** as an inevitable response to the **extremes** of **wealth** and **poverty** in capitalist society. They see the individual as "**forced**" into crime by the structure of society.

Crime, Deviance and Social Control

Traditional Marxists are Criticised for overlooking Other Effects on Crime

1) Traditional Marxists stated clearly that the cause of crime lay within the nature of the **capitalist system**. Their assumption that if you ended capitalism you'd end crime is **rejected** by many. There's **crime** in **socialist societies** like Cuba, and **some capitalist societies** such as Switzerland have very **low crime rates**.

2) Feminists accuse traditional Marxist theory of **ignoring** the role of **patriarchy** in rule creation and social control.

3) More recent Marxist-influenced theory such as left-realism (see glossary) reckons traditional Marxism focused too much on **corporate crime**. They dispute the argument that other crimes such as burglary are **insignificant**, especially as the **victims** are usually **working class**.

Radical Criminology argues criminals Choose to break the law

Taylor, Walton and Young's *The New Criminology* (1973) says crime is a choice

Background: *The New Criminology* was an attempt to present a thorough and considered **Marxist analysis** of crime, largely because Taylor, Walton and Young thought other Marxists, including Marx, had **failed** to do so. The main aim of *The New Criminology* was to move the sociology of crime on from the idea that society should be trying to **remove** deviant behaviour to a need to **understand** and **accept** it.

Theory: Taylor, Walton and Young argued that criminals were not **passive** individuals unable to control their economic situation as **traditional Marxists** had stated. Instead, crime was a **conscious**, **meaningful** and **deliberate choice** individuals made to try and **change society**.

Much crime is a **deliberate fight against capitalism**. Taylor, Walton and Young point to political action groups such as the **Black Panther** Movement who use criminal means to **agitate** the system. Robbery is also seen by the new criminologists as a potential means of **redistributing wealth**. (Robin Hood, anyone..)

Conclusion: Sociology needs a **"fully social theory of deviance"**. Deviance needs to be explained from **different viewpoints**, which consider how society is **organised** and at the same time **how** and **why** individuals **choose** to be deviant.

Seven Aspects of a full social theory of deviance, from Taylor, Walton and Young's *The New Criminology*.

1) How **wealth** and **power** are **distributed**.
2) The **unique circumstances** of each **individual act**.
3) The **nature** of the **deviant act** itself.
4) **Reactions** of the **rest of society** to the deviant act.
5) Who has the **power** to **make rules** about the **treatment** of deviance or **response** to deviance.
6) The **effect** being **labelled deviant** has on an individual.
7) How all these factors **interlink**.

Hall et al's (1978) study of the **moral panic** over **mugging** in Britain is a good example of a fully social theory of deviance in practice.

Hall et al analyse the **social** and **economic** and **political** conditions as well as the **motivations** of the **media** and the **government** and conclude that the **combination** of these factors all coming together at the same time led to a **moral panic**.

In brief: there was an <u>economic crisis</u> and a <u>crisis of hegemony</u> (unions and militants threatened state power), so the state wanted to exercise more control. The police <u>arrested more people</u>. The media picked up on this, and presented (black) muggers as a <u>threat to society</u>.

Practice Questions

Q1 Give two examples of how traditional Marxists argue capitalism creates crime.

Q2 According to Snider, how does the law protect ruling class crime?

Q3 According to Taylor, Walton and Young, why do people commit crime?

Exam Questions

Q1 Explain the Marxist view that the law is an instrument of the ruling class. (12 marks)

Q2 "The cause of crime lies in the structure of society not the nature of the individual." Consider this statement referring to at least two different sociological perspectives.

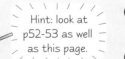
Hint: look at p52-53 as well as this page.

(40 marks)

It's not my fault — capitalism made me do it...

Again, not recommended as a defence in a court of law. It didn't work for me when I insisted on running naked through the streets. Anyway. It's the usual suspects here — Functionalists and Marxists. The Marxist theory of criminology is useful to learn. There are a lot of studies, and if you can explain and analyse them in the exam then you'll get plenty of marks.

Patterns of Crime

Crime is not equally distributed in the UK. There are age, gender, class and ethnicity differences.

Young people are Convicted of More Crime than Older People

Most crime is committed by teenagers. The peak age for criminal activity is 18 for men and 15 for women (**Social Trends, 33**).

1) It's argued that young people commit more crime because their **lifestyles** take them to **environments** where **crime takes place**. The vast majority of crime is **property theft** — young people are more likely to be on the **streets** or in **clubs**, which is where crimes like this (e.g. **pickpocketing** or **mugging**) often happen.

2) This is supported by the evidence that **young people** are most likely to be **victims** of crime too — if you're aged between 16-25 you're six times more likely to be a victim of crime than those aged 75 and older. It's not age itself, but the **likelihood** of being in areas where **opportunities for crime** arise which is the significant factor.

3) Young people may actually commit more crime, or it may be that they get **caught more** than older people. Crime committed by the **young** is typically more **visible**, e.g. vandalism, so it's likely to be witnessed, and the perpetrator is more likely to be caught. "White-collar crimes" such as **fraud** are more likely to be committed by **older people** but these offences are more **hidden** and don't take place in the public arena.

4) **Social stereotypes** that young people commit crime lead to police **suspecting** and **monitoring** young people more than older social groups — increasing their chances of being caught.

5) Young people are more likely to be **convicted** once in court — partly because they can't afford expensive **lawyer's fees**.

Men are Convicted of More Crime than Women

Women make up only **6%** of the prison population. (HM Prison Service)

58% of male prisoners released from prison are **re-convicted within 2 years**. (Social Trends, 1998)

In 2001, **167 per 10 000** of the **male** population were **found guilty** or **cautioned** for an offence compared to **3.7 per 10 000** of the female population.

1) Men are **suspected**, **charged** and **convicted** of crime of all types more than women. This pattern crosses **all other social factors** such as **age**, **class**, **ethnicity** and **region**.

2) The subcultural theories of **Miller (1962)** and **Merton (1968)** argue that the **culture** and **lifestyles** of **young men** encourage and lead to crime (remember, most crime is committed by the young).

3) **Heidensohn (1986)** says gender socialisation prompts men to be more **aggressive** which makes them more likely than women to commit violent crime. She also says that **women** are **socialised** into **not being criminal** in the same way as men are socialised into seeing criminal activity as acceptable. **Abbott and Wallace (1990)** argue young women are more closely watched by their families and given **less freedom** outside the home, reducing their **opportunities** for crime. Criminal behaviour would be seen as highly **deviant** as well as criminal for women.

4) **Ian Marsh (1986)** reckons that men commit more crime because they have more **opportunities** to do so. He said that where females have similar opportunities to males they seem **as likely** to break laws. An example of this is **handling stolen goods** — women have more opportunity to sell, buy or use stolen property than to steal goods in the first place.

5) There may be an **underestimation** of female crime because the police and courts are **less likely** to **suspect** women or give women a **custodial sentence**. The stereotypes of men as criminal work as a form of **sexism** against men, which allows female criminal activity to go **unchecked**. **Campbell (1981)** did a **self-report survey** which unearthed a lot **more female crime** than the official statistics. However, she did include more trivial crimes than the official statistics do.

Urban areas have much More Crime than Rural ones

In 2003-2004, Metropolitan (urban) police forces recorded 43% of all crime.

In 2002, less than 2% of people living in rural areas became victims of burglary.

In 2003-2004, 60% of all robbery in the UK took place in three urban areas (London, Manchester and West Midlands).

This table shows the percentage of households which have been **victims** (at least once) of **vehicle theft**, **burglary** and **violent crime**. The data's from the British Crime Survey, 2004.

There's **more crime** in **cities**.

Area type	All vehicle theft	All burglary	All violent crime
Inner city	15.3	5.3	5.8
Urban (towns and outer part of city)	10.3	3.3	4.4
All non-rural (cities, towns, suburbs)	10.8	3.6	4.6
Rural	6.5	1.9	2.7
All households/all adults	9.7	3.2	4.1

Sociologists argue most crime takes place in cities because there are more **opportunities** to be involved in crime in cities. Higher density populations mean more chances for **robbery** and **property crime**. Most young people live in urban areas and they are the most likely to commit crime. It's hard for criminals to remain anonymous in close-knit rural **communities**.

Patterns of Crime

Most criminal convictions are of people with a **Working Class Background**

There are more **working class** people in **prison** than any other social class. Home Office figures also show that the majority of people who appear in **court** are working class, regardless of whether they're found guilty or not.

The idea of an upper class person in prison is so rare and contrary to cultural norms, that a Lord convicted of fraud can find himself on a "celebrity" reality TV show.

1) **Sub-cultural theorists** such as **Miller** argue this reflects the working class sub-cultures which often have crime as an accepted or rewarded activity.

2) **Marxists** argue the system of law and order is run by the **ruling class**, against the interests of the working class. They say parts of the working class are criminalised by a biased system — see p.50-51.

3) Middle class crime is treated more leniently by society. Fraud and white collar crime is often undetected and seen as "victimless crime" by the public. Consider public response to benefit fraud compared to tax or insurance fraud. There's more about **Marxist** opinions of why this is on p.50-51.

An **Ethnic Minority Background** increases your chances of arrest and conviction

	Population of the UK	Police "stop and search" England and Wales	Arrests for serious offences, England and Wales	Male prison population	Female prison population
White	92%	74.3%	84.3%	75.7%	69.1%
Asian	4%	7.3%	4.8%	3.4%	0.8%
Black	2%	14.6%	8.8%	16%	25.3%
Mixed and Other	2%	3.7%	2.1%	4.8%	4.7%

2001 census, and the Home Office "Statistics on Race and the Criminal Justice System" (2004)

1) Some have argued that **police racism** results in higher suspicion against black people in general. The Macpherson Report (1999) concluded that the police were institutionally racist. The court system has also been accused of automatically favouring white middle class defendants. There are few black people in either the police force or the legal system.

The stop and search, arrest and prison figures are based on <u>what a person looks like</u>. The census records what a person <u>identifies themselves</u> as.

2) **Hall et al (1978)** and **Gilroy (1987)** argue that young black people have been labelled as criminal by modern British society and have become a **scapegoat** for social problems in society.

3) Hall also says that high levels of **unemployment** among young black men leads some young black men to **opt out** of **mainstream society** and turn to **crime**.

Similar in some ways, but Hall blames the system and New Right theorists blame the person.

4) New Right sociologists favour a **subcultural** explanation for the differences.

5) **Ethnic minority** households are **more at risk of crime** than other households — e.g. the British Crime Survey says they're more likely to be mugged than white groups, and slightly more likely to be victims of vehicle theft. Pakistanis and Bangladeshis were more likely to be **burgled**. The survey found ethnic minority respondents were **more worried about crime** in 2000 than white respondents.

Only **23% of reported crimes** in 2003 were **solved** — i.e. someone was convicted for the offence in 2003 (2004 Social Trends). The social profile of who committed the **unsolved** and **undetected** crimes could change these patterns considerably.

Practice Questions

Q1   Which social groups are most likely to be convicted of crime in Britain?

Q2   What evidence is there that crime is more prevalent in urban areas?

Q3   Briefly state the two explanations that Stuart Hall gives for increased arrest and criminality among the black population.

Exam Question

Q1   Examine sociological explanations for 76% of the UK male prison population being white.   (12 marks)

Avoid committing crime — be an old woman and live in the countryside...

Of course, that's easier said than done for many of us, particularly young men. But just because a task is difficult does not mean you shouldn't strive to achieve it. Being young, male, working class, black and living in an urban area puts you at the highest risk of being convicted, or of being a victim, of crime. There are loads of possible reasons for this — make sure you understand them.

Social Reactions to Crime and Deviance

Social Action theorists (Interactionists) say that social reaction is really what defines deviance in the first place. Great.

Interactionists say that Deviant folk aren't really Different from everyone else

1) Interactionist study of crime and deviance starts from the standpoint that deviants are **not characteristically different** from the rest of the population. They are deviant because their chosen behaviour is **labelled deviant** by others in society. Interactionists believe that deviance is **socially constructed**.

Interactionists are also called social action theorists.

2) Interactionists stress the idea that deviance is **relative** — it varies over time and place as values, norms and social expectations change. For example, 100 years ago, it was deviant for women to wear trousers.

3) Also, what's **deviant** for some groups in society is **conformity** for others. **Subcultures** have **different norms** to mainstream society.

4) The **same behaviour** gets **different reactions** depending on the social situation. For example, **nudity** is normal and acceptable in the privacy of your own home but seen as deviant (and criminal) in a public space.

Becker (1963) argues deviance is behaviour which has been **labelled deviant** by the **reaction of others**.

He said that the **reaction** of those around you is what makes you **recognise** your behaviour as deviant. Becker said "Deviance is not a quality that lies in the **behaviour** itself but in the **interaction** between the person who commits an act, and those who respond to it."

Social Action theorists like Becker were the first sociologists to **challenge the assumption** that sociologists should focus on what **causes** people to act in deviant and criminal ways. Instead, they studied how an act or behaviour comes to be **labelled as deviant** by the rest of society, and the **consequences** of that label or reaction.

Being Labelled as Deviant can Affect Future Behaviour

Interactionists argue we form our self-identity from **interpreting** how others respond to us and **internalising** the reaction. A **label** has a **positive** or **negative** effect on the individual and it helps to define them in their **own eyes** as well as in others' eyes. Becker calls this a "**self concept**".

1) Becker argued that a **self concept** of being deviant can **increase deviant behaviour**. For example, if a person is **shamed** by the reaction of others who know they have been in trouble with the police, they may return to criminal activity or **join a criminal group** to escape the rejection they feel. This then reinforces the label of criminal and it becomes even harder to remove and a bigger part of their identity. Becker called this process the **deviant career**.

2) The **label** of **criminal** is **not easily removed** by society, whatever the actions of the individual — it becomes their **master status** (see glossary). On release from prison many individuals find it hard to obtain work, housing and positions of trust because of the reaction of others to their status as an **ex-offender**.

3) **Jock Young (1971)** used his study of drug users in Notting Hill to demonstrate the process of becoming deviant.

The marijuana users developed a **deviant self concept** because their drug of choice was **illegal**.	The **deviant** element became their **main identity** in society. They were "hippies" first and foremost.	The **negative response** of those around them and the police made the drug-taking more **significant** to their lives.	Their drug-taking **increased**.

4) **Goffman (1961)** wrote about a deviant career in **mental illness**. He said the **negative label** of being **mad** is **imposed** on the patient by society and psychiatry, and that the patient must eventually **conform** to it.

Lemert (1951) distinguished between Primary and Secondary deviance

Primary deviance = the initial deviant act.

Secondary deviance = deviant acts committed after the individual has **accepted the label** of deviant.

1) Lemert argued **most people** commit some acts of **primary deviance** in their lives but that it was of **little significance**.

2) When there's a **societal reaction** (a reaction from society as a whole or groups within society such as family, peers, police and the media) the individual is **labelled** as **deviant**.

3) Lemert argues that when the individual **feels the weight** of the label "deviant" or "criminal", they sometimes commit **more** of the deviant behaviour. For example, once a person is labelled an **alcoholic**, they might drink more because well, they're an alcoholic, and alcoholics drink. Lemert called this **secondary deviance**.

Public reaction to an individual labelled deviant can be very powerful. Sometimes, individuals **commit suicide** once their deviance has been discovered — e.g. it's not uncommon for suspects in Internet child pornography raids to kill themselves.

Social Reactions to Crime and Deviance

Critics argue people are not as Passive as Interactionists suggest

1) **Ronald Akers (1967)** criticises both Becker and Lemert for presenting individuals as **powerless** to make decisions or take control of their own identity. **Deviance**, according to **Akers**, is not something which **happens** to people but a **choice** that individuals make.

2) **Taylor, Walton and Young (1973)** argue many forms of behaviour are **widely viewed** as deviant — so deviants **know** they are breaking the law or social rules **before** any **societal reaction** but they **still do it**.

3) Marxist critics accuse interactionism of **ignoring the role of power** in defining crime and deviance. Certain groups have the **power** to influence what is classified as **criminal** or **socially unacceptable**.

4) **Gouldner (1973)** accused interactionists of being **fascinated with deviance**, and even suggests they enjoy observing "cool" deviants, and hanging out with the "underworld". He thinks interactionists aren't interested in changing society.

The Media plays a powerful role in Amplifying Deviance in society

Interactionists such as **Stanley Cohen (1972)** argue the media helps to **create** the deviance it predicts or anticipates.

The Amplification of Deviance

1) Media presents a **distorted view** of the level of crime.
2) This distorted view creates **public concern**.
3) Related pieces of crime and deviance are **over-reported** and given more prominence than they'd otherwise have.
4) This keeps the issue or problem **high** on the **public agenda**.
5) The public want **something done** about the problem.
6) The police are more **aware** or sensitive to the problem so they **discover more crime**.
7) Police records **reinforce** the idea that there is **more crime** and **deviance**.

1) The risk of being a victim of crime is **amplified** by over-reporting by the media. This creates a public response of **panic** or **outrage**. Cohen refers to this as a **moral panic**.

Definition of a **moral panic**: "When a **condition, episode, person** or **group** of persons emerges to become **defined** as a **threat** to **societal values** and interests." **Stanley Cohen.**

2) Cohen famously developed his theory from a study of conflicts between **Mods and Rockers** in 1964, but there are plenty of **new** examples, especially with the increased power of the media — e.g. gun crime, "bogus asylum seekers", benefit fraud, Roma (Gypsy) encampments.

3) The state response to a moral panic in society is to introduce **stricter** forms of **social control** through legislation.

4) **Hall et al (1978)** claim that the national concern about **mugging** in the early 1970s was a **moral panic**. The media claimed that mugging was a new kind of crime, but Hall et al point out that violent street robbery had been going on for a long time, and wasn't rising particularly fast at the time of the moral panic.

Practice Questions

Q1 Why are interactionists less interested in the causes of crime than other sociologists?
Q2 Explain how the reactions of others are significant in the interactionist understanding of deviance.
Q3 What is "amplification of deviance"?
Q4 Define the term "moral panic".

Exam Questions

Q1 To what extent does the media play a significant role in creating deviance in society? (40 marks)

Q2 Evaluate the view that societal reaction is a major cause of deviance. (40 marks)

Sigh. If you will insist on running naked through the streets...

It's interesting how people react to deviant behaviour. Some people scream and shout, others run away, and others pretend it's not happening. Well, according to Becker and his merry bunch of interactionists, it's the reaction that people have to deviance that makes it deviant. They even went as far as saying that reaction can make deviance more deviant. Give a dog a bad name...

Suicide

There's an awful lot of sociology on suicide, for two reasons. Firstly, it's a totally individual act, so it's a big task for sociology to explain. Secondly, it's been a focus for exploring issues of sociological methodology since Durkheim used his study of suicide to explain the "rules" of sociological research and enquiry. So all this ties in with Section Four.

Durkheim's study of Suicide is one of the most Important Sociological Works of all time

Durkheim wrote in the **1890s**, and was one of the very **first sociologists** — right at the forefront of establishing and defining sociology as a scientific discipline. Durkheim argued that it was not only **possible** to apply **scientific principles** to **social phenomena** but that it was **essential** to apply scientific principles in order to produce **useful sociology**. His 1897 book *Suicide: a study in sociology*, uses his scientific methods to explore suicide.

1) Durkheim chose suicide **deliberately**, because as the most **individual**, **private** and **psychologically driven** act it was considered by most **not** to be a **social** phenomenon.

2) If sociology **could** identify **social factors** and **causes** of suicide, this would demonstrate the **power** and **impact** of **society** on **individual behaviour**.

3) Durkheim followed the **methodology** laid down in his earlier book, *The Rules of Sociological Method*, in his suicide study. This methodology was **rigorous**, **systematic**, **detailed** and **scientific** analysis.

4) Durkheim said that if this **scientific methodology** is followed then "**social facts**" can be discovered in the same way as **scientific** research reveals **laws** or **facts** of the **natural world**.

Analysis of Statistics found some groups were More Likely to Commit Suicide

1) Durkheim's analysis of the **official statistics** on suicide revealed some **social groups** were **more likely** to commit suicide than others. He looked at a large amount of data from **different societies** and from **different cultural** and **social groups** within the same society.

2) Social **patterns** of **suicide** rates demonstrate suicide is **not a random individual act**. **Social factors** play a part.

> **Correlation between suicide and other "social facts".**
> * Suicide rates were higher in predominantly **Protestant** countries than in **Catholic** ones.
> * **Jews** were the religious group with the **lowest suicide** rate.
> * **Married** people were **less likely** to commit suicide.
> * **Low suicide rates** were found in countries after a **national upheaval** or **crisis**.
> * Those with more **education** had a **higher suicide rate**.

Durkheim used "social facts" (statistics) as his raw data and then analysed the data to draw conclusions on the cause of suicide. He didn't question the reliability or accuracy of the statistics — that all came later...

Durkheim concluded there were Four Forms of Suicide

Durkheim concluded there were four different forms of suicide, related to how much **integration** and **regulation** there was in a society.

Social integration means **socialisation** into the **norms**, **values** and **lifestyles** of social groups and society.

Moral regulation means the **control** that **society** and **social groups** have over an **individual's behaviour**.

Durkheim's **four types of suicide** relate to **dysfunctional** integration or regulation.

Form of suicide	Cause	Example
Egoistic	**Not enough integration.** The individual isn't successfully integrated into groups or society.	More suicide in Protestants compared to Catholics because Protestants had a **looser social network/belief system**.
Anomic	**Not enough regulation.** Society has insufficient control over individuals.	Often in periods of **economic depression** or **very rapid expansion**, the suicide rate rises. People find it hard to adapt.
Altruistic	**Too much integration.** An over-integrated individual sacrifices their life for the group.	**Followers** who commit suicide after the death of their **leader**. Terrorist **suicide bombers** are a modern example.
Fatalistic	**Too much regulation.** The individual is too highly controlled by society.	Suicides of **prisoners** or **slaves**.

Durkheim has been Criticised by other Positivist Sociologists

Positivists try to use scientific methods.
See p.38-39

Halbwachs (1930) largely supported Durkheim's conclusions but he pointed out that the impact of **rural** versus **urban** lifestyles on suicide rates hadn't been considered.

Gibbs and Martin (1964) argued that Durkheim hadn't used vigorous enough scientific methods even though he'd stressed how important they were. The key concepts of **integration** and **regulation** weren't **defined** closely enough to be **measured statistically**. Gibbs and Martin query how anyone can **know** what "**normal**" levels of integration and regulation are.

Suicide

Interactionist Sociologists have devised Alternative Theories of Suicide

Interactionist sociologists say social reality isn't a series of "social facts" for sociologists to discover, but a series of different **meanings** and **interpretations** that each person brings to and takes from each situation.

Durkheim's work is **fatally flawed** from this perspective because he relies on the **unquestioning** use of official **statistics**. According to interactionists, **statistics aren't fact** — they're a **social construction** based on the definitions of the people who compile them. In other words, statistics give you **one picture** of society, not the **only picture**.

Douglas (1967) said there was a need to categorise suicides according to their **social meanings** because the **triggers** and **response** to suicide are **different** in **different cultures**.

Douglas identified **four social meanings** for suicides in modern industrial societies.

1) **Transformation** of the **soul**.
2) **Transformation** of the **self**.
3) Achieving **sympathy**.
4) Achieving **revenge**.

Baechler (1979) used **case studies** for his research into the meanings behind suicides. He concluded suicide was an action **chosen** by individuals to **solve a problem** when all other solutions had **failed**. Suicide is one response to the social circumstances an individual is in.

He also established four main types of suicide.

1) **Escapist** — an attempt to **remove oneself** from an **unbearable** situation.
2) **Aggressive** — a means of harming or **hurting** other people.
3) **Oblative** — a means to **achieve a wish**, such as to join a loved one who's already dead.
4) **Ludic** — **knowingly taking risks** likely to result in death.

Atkinson suggests the key question is "How do deaths get Categorised as suicide?"

There is a **social process** involved in a death becoming **labelled** as a **suicide**.

1) **Atkinson (1978)** studied coroners' courts and suggested that coroners use their own **interpretations** and **definitions** in order to define a death as **suicide**.
2) He thought that coroners had a "**typical biography**" of a suicide victim to compare the case against — the more factors **fitted**, the more likely they'd record the death as suicide. For example, **young single men** were more likely to be labelled suicide than **middle-aged married men**.
3) Atkinson concludes suicide statistics are **not facts** but reflections of **coroners' interpretations**.

Coroners don't have to record a death as suicide, murder or accident. They can record an open verdict if they aren't 100% sure.

Critics of Atkinson have said that although the suicide statistics are **socially constructed** they follow a **clear set of criteria** which are **shared** and therefore there will be **consistency** in the figures.

Practice Questions

Q1 What are the two reasons why the study of suicide is so important to sociology as a discipline?
Q2 What did Durkheim mean by "regulation" and "integration" in society?
Q3 What does Atkinson suggest about the social construction of suicide?

Exam Questions

Q1 Evaluate the importance of Durkheim's study of suicide within the discipline of sociology. (40 marks)

Q2 Assess the view that suicide statistics tell us more about the values and interpretations of coroners than they reveal about the causes of suicide. (40 marks)

On a more cheerful note, section five has just ended...

This all ties in with the stuff on sociological method in Section Four. Suicide, although a terrible downer, is something that sociologists find deeply fascinating. Never let it be said that sociologists aren't an odd bunch. The key is to understand Durkheim's theory, where he got his data from, and why he's criticised by interactionists. It could well be on the exam...

Social Class and Occupation

This section is a "synoptic" module, which means the examiners expect you to make links between this topic and other topics you have studied in Sociology. That includes topics you studied for AS, as well as A2.

Societies are Stratified — divided into Layers

Stratification means the way societies are divided into **layers**. The **richest** and **most powerful** are at the **top**, the **poorest** and **most powerless** are at the **bottom**. In between are lots of **strata** (layers, like the layers in rock) organised in a **hierarchy**.

A **stratified** society can contain inequalities of **status**, **income**, **class**, **religion**, **ethnicity**, **gender** and **age**.

Social class is the main stratification system in **modern**, **Western capitalist societies** like the **UK**. Social class is partly based on **economic** factors — **jobs**, **income** and **wealth**. Social class also has elements of **power** and **prestige**.

Other stratification systems include the caste system as used in India, and the feudal system as used in medieval Britain.

Sociologists often talk about Four Social Classes in the UK

1) The **upper class** are **wealthy** and **powerful**. The original upper class was the **landowning aristocracy**. Their wealth is **passed on from generation to generation**. People who have made a lot of money from business or from the entertainment industry are also sometimes considered to be upper class.

2) The **middle class** earn their money from **non-manual work**. Teachers, doctors, managers and pretty much anyone who **earns their living sitting in an office** are middle class. The middle class is **getting bigger** because there are **more non-manual jobs** these days, and fewer manual jobs.

3) The **working class** make their money from **manual work**. Farm labourers and factory workers are working class. The working class have **poorer life chances** than the middle class.

4) The **underclass** get their money from **state benefits**. They include the long-term unemployed and the homeless. The underclass have **the poorest life chances**.

Sociologists have most often focused on the division between the middle class and the working class.

See p.62 for more on Marxist stratification.

Marx divided society into just Two Social Classes

1) The **proletariat** (workers) produce goods of economic value. According to Marx, they don't own the means of production — all they own and control is their own labour power.

2) The **bourgeoisie** (bosses) own the means of production. Marx said they exploit workers in order to generate profit.

3) There wasn't a clearly defined **middle class** at the time when Marx was writing his economic theories.

Relating Class to Occupation poses Problems

1) Occupation does bring **status** and **prestige** with it. People **judge** each other by the jobs they do.

2) Two individuals in the **same occupational class** can have very different **income** and **prestige** status — e.g. a highly paid consultant neurologist compared to a low paid junior doctor.

3) Basing class entirely on occupation misses out most of the **upper class** — a lot of them **don't have jobs** as such, but live off **rental income** from property, and income from **share ownership**.

A good social class scheme must **represent** what people in society **really think** about the **status** that goes with each occupational class — it must be **devised** and **tested** by **research**. There are far **too many occupations** for a research sample to say what they think of them **all**, so sociologists usually ask individuals about 20 or so **common** and **representative occupations**. They make inferences about the rest of the occupations in society — which is the tricky bit.

The Government used to use a scale of Five Classes called the RG scale

1) This scale is called the **Registrar General's Scale** (RG scale), and was used until 2000.

2) The **never employed** aren't included, and **unemployed** people are classified according to their **last job**.

3) The RG scale is based on the **head of household's** occupation (usually the man).

4) **Married women** were classified according to their **husband's job** — this was **sexist**.

5) Also, because the RG scale only considered the head of household's job, it didn't matter what kind of job **other people in the home** had. For example, it **wouldn't distinguish** between a household made up of **two lawyers** and a household made up of a **lawyer** and a **cleaner**.

6) There can be **huge variations** in **income** and **life chances** between different occupations within a class.

Class	Example
I) Professional	Lawyer, accountant, doctor
II) Intermediate	Teacher, nurse, manager
III) skilled non-manual	Office worker, sales assistant
III) skilled manual	Electrician, plumber
IV) semi-skilled manual	Postman
V) unskilled manual	Labourer, refuse collector, cleaner

middle class { I), II), III) skilled non-manual }
working class { III) skilled manual, IV), V) }

"Head of household" meant highest male earner, or if no male, highest female earner.

Social Class and Occupation

The Government now uses a scale of Eight Classes called the NS-SEC

Since 2000, the **government** has used a new scale — the **National Statistics Socio-Economic Classification** (**NS-SEC**).
The NS-SEC has **eight classes** based on type of **employment**, rather than **skill level**:

1) **higher managerial and professional**	Lawyer, doctor, company director
2) **lower managerial and professional**	Nurse, social worker, police officer
3) **intermediate**	Secretary, personal assistant, paramedic
4) **small employers and self-employed**	Owner of a restaurant, self employed plumber
5) **lower supervisory and technical**	Builder's foreman, sales floor supervisor in a shop
6) **semi-routine**	Postman, receptionist, sales assistant in a shop
7) **routine**	Waitress, van driver, farm labourer, cleaner
8) **never worked and long term unemployed**	last worked more than a year ago

Class 1 can be divided into a) large employers and managers, and b) higher professional.

The NS-SEC is derived from Goldthorpe's social class scheme — see below.

1) The NS-SEC is based on three areas:

- **Employment relations** — whether someone is an **employer**, **self-employed** or **employed**, whether they're **salaried** or paid a **weekly wage**, and how large an organisation they work in. *This is Weberian — see p.63.*
- **Labour market situation** — income, benefits and job security, promotion prospects.
- **Work situation** — where the person is in the **workplace hierarchy**, and how much **control** they have at work.

2) The RG was replaced by the NS-SEC because of the recent changes in **employment patterns**. There were fewer **manual** workers and far more workers in **service industries**, so **skill level** was no longer a good way to classify workers.

3) The NS-SEC takes into account changes in social position of some occupations (e.g. shop assistants).

4) Each **individual worker** is classified, rather than classifying a whole **household** by one person's job.

5) The NS-SEC still doesn't account for the "idle rich" — wealthy **upper class** people who don't need jobs.

Goldthorpe's Scheme has Seven Classes

1) In the 1970s, Goldthorpe (a Weberian) based his social classification on **market situation** and **work situation**. He adapted it in the 1980s to include employment relations.

2) Goldthorpe used this scale in his Oxford Mobility study — there's more about it on p.68.

I)	**upper service class**	lawyer, doctor, large employer
II)	**lower service class**	teacher, nurse, manager
III)	**routine non-manual class**	secretary, personal assistant
IV)	**petty bourgeoisie**	self employed, small employers
V)	**lower technical, supervisors**	foreman, dental hygienist
VI)	**skilled manual class**	bricklayer, electrician (employed)
VII)	**unskilled manual class**	waitress, labourer, cleaner

Wright's Scheme combines Marxism with Bureaucracy

1) **Erik Olin Wright's** (1985, 1990, 1997) scheme has a traditional **Marxist** divide between **owners** and **employees**.

2) It also classifies employees in two dimensions — firstly, whether they're **managers**, **supervisors** or **workers**, and secondly whether they've got **skills and qualifications** or not.

Practice Questions

Q1 Give one problem of using occupation to measure class.

Q2 What class was missing from the Registrar General's scale?

Q3 Give an example of a semi-routine occupation from the NS-SEC scheme.

Q4 What class would a self-employed electrician be in the Goldthorpe scheme?

Exam Question

Q1 Assess the validity of judging social class solely on occupation.   (40 marks)

Oh how I wish this was a classless society — there'd be less to learn...

What a lot of class schemes. For the bare basics, learn the NS-SEC, the RG, and the differences between them. If you want to look like you're really on the ball, you can mention that class/occupation schemes can be Marxist (based on economics and income) or Weberian (based on labour market position and employment relations). The NS-SEC is well Weberian. Innit.

Theories of Stratification

There's no dispute that power, status and economic assets aren't equally distributed within society. There is an awful lot of debate about why. A sociologist's answer depends on their fundamental beliefs about the nature of society. Off we go again...

Functionalists *say the* Class System *helps society to* Run Smoothly

1) Functionalism says that society is a meritocracy — the most able people rise to the top.

2) Fundamental to **Functionalism** (try saying that quickly...) is the **strong belief** that the class system enables each individual to find their **right place** and **role** in society.

3) Functionalists say that the **most important** positions in society must be filled by the brightest and most able people.

4) According to **Functionalism**, the people who do well in terms of the common values of society will be at the top of the stratification system. High **status**, **power** and high income are **rewards** for conforming to society's values.

5) Most people **don't object** to people in powerful positions getting **extra status** and **rewards**. According to functionalists, this shows that they support the values which underpin the system.

Talcott Parsons was an influential Functionalist

1) Parsons established the Functionalist position that stratification is **inevitable** and **useful** in all societies.

2) He argued that stratification systems **evaluate** individuals in terms of **common social values** — high status is a reward for **conforming** to society's values.

3) In Parsons' view, stratification **reinforces** the **collective goals** of society and establishes **order**.

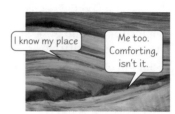

I know my place

Me too. Comforting, isn't it.

I doubt Parsons was thinking about strata in rock...

Davis and Moore (1945) argue that without a stratification system, society would break down

1) According to Davis and Moore, stratification has the function of **role allocation**. It makes sure the most able and talented do the most important jobs.

2) **Inequality in reward** (pay) and **status** are essential to **motivate** the best individuals to take on the most important roles and jobs. These roles usually require long periods of training. High rewards compensate people for spending a long time in education and training.

This argument may sound familiar — it's often used to justify high rewards given to company directors and even famous sports stars.

Functionalists *have been accused of* Overlooking *the* "Uneven Playing Field"

1) **Tumin (1953)** is the **most important critic** of Davis and Moore. He pointed out that individuals with the same talent and ability don't have an equal chance to "reach the top". He says that this **inequality of opportunity** is **overlooked** by Davis and Moore.

2) **Tumin** also criticises the functionalist concept of some roles being more "functionally important" than others. It's not clear who can decide **which jobs** are **more important** than others. Some of the essential jobs in society such as nursing, teaching and childcare are paid considerably less than some less useful jobs such as advertising, PR and entertainment.

3) Also, Tumin said that Davis and Moore ignore the influence of **power** on rewards. **Pay inequality** may be to do with differences in **bargaining power**, rather than difference in usefulness.

4) Tumin wasn't having any truck with the idea that stratification **motivates** people, either. He thought that social stratification can be a barrier to motivation. The **lower** a person's social class, the **more likely** they are to **leave school** without good qualifications, and the **less likely** they are to be **motivated** to chase a **high status** position.

5) High status groups can put up **barriers to entry** — using their power to restrict access to the group. This allows them to set a high market price for their services.

6) Davis and Moore assume that the **number** of people who are **talented enough** to fill high status jobs is (curiously) **identical** to the number of high status jobs up for grabs. There's actually **no evidence** for this. The pool of talent could be much larger than Functionalists think it is.

7) Functionalists **ignore** the negative aspects of stratification. Stratification is a system of haves and have nots. People in the bottom strata can feel excluded from society. Stratification can actually divide society rather than integrating it.

Theories of Stratification

The **New Right** argue that the **Social Stratification** system is **Unequal** but **Fair**

New Right thinking became popular in the 1980s. It's based on **19th century liberalism**, which saw the **free market** as the **best** way of sorting out everything in society from boredom to backache. The New Right say **governments shouldn't intervene in the market** or promote equality as this takes away motivation for people to **pull themselves up by their bootstraps**.

New Right thinking is sometimes known as **neo-functionalism** (or political functionalism) because it pursues the same themes.

1) **Peter Saunders (1990)** is a key British New Right sociologist. **Saunders** argues that societies with stratification systems based on economic differences aren't inevitable (as Parsons thought) but they are a good idea.

2) Saunders says **stratification** is a good idea because **unequal rewards motivate** people to **work hard**. He says that in a society with equal rewards, some people wouldn't pull their weight. He sees physical force as the only alternative to unequal rewards — and obviously prefers unequal rewards.

3) Saunders says that **inequality** promotes **economic growth**. Individuals are motivated to **start businesses** so that they can make money, which **benefits society** by creating **jobs** and **wealth**. He points to the rise in small businesses and entrepreneurs in modern society to demonstrate how anyone can do well if they work hard enough.

4) New Right thinkers like Saunders believe in legal equality and equality of opportunity, rather than equality of outcome. Saunders says that it's more important for society to be a meritocracy than for society to be equal.

5) In a **free market**, market forces control who earns what, according to **supply of talent** and **demand for talent**. People whose skills are highly **demanded**, but in short **supply**, can earn a lot of money. A system based on the free market is **unequal** (some people earn a lot more than others) but it's **fair** according to New Right thinkers because every individual can try to be successful in the market place.

1) **Saunders (1996)** sees Britain as pretty **close** to being a **meritocracy**. He thinks that **economic rewards** match up with **merit** and **ability**.

2) He argues that what **looks** like **inequality of opportunity** between middle class and working class is actually caused by **inequality of ability** and **effort**. In other words, he thinks that middle class children **deserve** better jobs because they're more able, and they work harder.

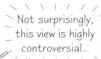
Not surprisingly, this view is highly controversial...

Critics of **Functionalism** and **New Right** theory point out **Social Problems**

1) **Gordon Marshall** and **Adam Swift (1993)** say that capitalist societies are not as **meritocratic** as the New Right claim.

2) They argue the **free market** does not guarantee a **fair chance** for all. Opportunities vary according to which class you are born into — for example, inherited wealth plays a large part in starting small businesses. **Luck** can play a part in success, too.

3) Evidence also shows that people from **working class** backgrounds have **less chance** than upper class people of getting top jobs — even when they have the **same educational qualifications**. **Class** still plays a part even when people have **equal ability**.

4) They also criticise functionalists for largely ignoring **social problems** such as **poverty**, which result from the stratification system.

Practice Questions

Q1 In what way did Parsons say that stratification was useful for society?

Q2 Explain what Davis and Moore mean by role allocation.

Q3 Why does Saunders say stratification is a good idea?

Q4 Give one criticism of New Right thinking on stratification.

Exam Questions

Q1 Examine the view that social inequality is an inevitable product of a successful society. (12 marks)

Q2 "Modern Britain is a meritocratic society." Discuss with reference to one or more of the following topics: education; work and leisure; health; families and households. (40 marks)

<u>New Wrong thinking had even more critics than usual...</u>

There's a pattern to Sociology teaching at A-level: you study the main theories about each topic and then evaluate and compare them... It's a good approach because it teaches you to look at topics from different points of view. It can get a bit repetitive though. Functionalist, Marxist and Interactionist views come up over and over again. What about Zoroastrian views? Huh?

Theories of Stratification

Surprise — some more theories of stratification! Sorry, I should have warned you on the last page. That was a cruel trick.

Marxists *see stratification as a* Deliberately Divisive *tool for* Exploiting *workers*

1) For Marx, **class** was the key to understanding **absolutely everything** in society. And I mean e-v-e-r-y-t-h-i-n-g.

2) Class emerges in a society which can **produce more** than it **needs** to. Marx called this extra production "**surplus value**" and argued that it was the class who **controlled** this **surplus value** that controlled **society**.

3) Marx argued there are **only two classes** (strata) in society — the **proletariat** and the **bourgeoisie**. For Marx, a class is a **social group** who share the **same relationship** to the means of **production**.

Producers	Proletariat or subject class	Majority	Only own their labour	Poor
Non-producers	Bourgeoisie or ruling class	Minority	Own the means of production	Wealthy

The ruling class own the means of production

1) Those who own the means of production can control both the **price** at which they **sell** the goods produced, and the **wages** they pay those who produce the goods.

2) It's only by paying the workers **less** than they **sell** the goods for that they can make a **profit**. It is this profit which gives them the **wealth** and **power** to **control** the rest of society in their own interests.

The subject class are the producers

1) They **don't own** the means of production. They only own their **labour**. Because they only own their labour power they have **very little control** in society.

2) They're **completely dependent** on the **ruling class** for **wages** to live on.

1) Marx argued that all other forms of power come from **economic** power.

2) Marxism says the **education** system, **legal** system, **police** and **media** are all instruments of ruling class power. This is because those with **economic power** also have the power to **shape** and **control** the institutions in society. According to Marxism, all these institutions serve to keep the subject class in its place — powerless.

3) The ruling class also use **institutions** in society to **control ideas** and **values** in society — via the **dominant ideology**. For example, the notion that capitalist society is meritocratic and anyone can get to the top is a "false truth" according to Marxism. **Institutions** in society such as education spread this idea, and everyone's happy in the belief that society is fair. This is **useful to the ruling class** — it prevents workers from rising up and starting a revolution.

Marx thought that Workers *should have a* Revolution *and bring in* Communism

Marx thought society could be **equal** if the **means of production** were owned by **everyone**, so everyone benefited rather than a few. He was certain this would be the end result of capitalism — workers would eventually realise their power and strength, and overthrow the ruling class in a **revolution**, creating a new equal society which Marx called **communism**.

The 20th century saw the **start** and **end** of some large scale communist societies such as the USSR. The **failure** of these communist societies, and the high levels of both **corruption** and **inequality in communist societies** have caused many sociologists to say that Marx was wrong and **egalitarian societies aren't possible**. Modern Marxists argue that the USSR and China **weren't true communism**.

China is still officially communist, but it's adopted "capitalism with Chinese characteristics", a mixture of both ideologies.

Neo-Marxist *theories of stratification try to explain the* Middle Class

In traditional Marxism, there's **no middle class**. There clearly **is** a **middle class** in **modern society**, and modern Marxists have grappled with different ways of explaining it.

1) **Erik Olin Wright (1978, 1989)** developed a Marxist analysis of class which explained the middle class of salaried professionals which grew in the late 20th century. This group have some control over the means of production, and may own bits of it but they don't control large sections of labour power. This group is called the **petty bourgeoisie**.

2) Wright says these individuals may experience "**contradictory class locations**" — they have **things in common** with **both** classes at **different** times. For example, they may own shares (part-ownership of modern means of production) but may also lose their livelihood at the will of the ruling class (e.g. if they lose their job, or the share price falls).

3) Wright concludes that **class conflict** and **exploitation** are more **complicated** in the late 20th (and now 21st) century than Marx predicted but class is **still** the basis of power and wealth in society.

4) **Edgell (1993)** accuses Wright of leaving Marx behind and having more in common with **Weber**.

The **key message** from neo-Marxists is: **don't dismiss Marx's theory completely** just because he didn't mention a middle class.

Theories of Stratification

Weber argued Class is "Unequal Access to Material Resources"

Weber considered many of the same issues as Marx. Like Marx, he argued class and stratification come from an **economic** basis. Unlike Marx, he didn't go into any detailed predictions about the future, or analysis of the past.

Weber said that there are **three distinct areas** or forms of **stratification** in modern society.

Class power	Economic power to access material goods and resources in society.
Social power	Status and prestige, and being respected by others.
Party power	Political power and ability to influence decision-making.

These tend to be **interlinked** in real life — a person with **social power** is also likely to have **political** and **economic** power.

1) **Weber** concentrated on class power. He argued that an individual's **class power** and **class position** derives from their market position — i.e. their **economic chances**, and their ability to **control** their **wages** and **working conditions**.

2) An individual's **market position** varies partly depending on how in **demand** their skills and talents are — i.e. how much an employer is willing to pay for their services. Be careful though — market position isn't just an individual's ability to get a job. It also covers their **ownership** of **property** and **assets** (e.g. shares).

3) Stratification isn't a case of **two classes** opposed to each other (Marx) or a **competitive meritocracy** (Functionalism and New Right) but a **complex** hierarchy of layers, each with their own class or market position.

Neo-Weberian Theory influences modern Class Schemes

The big name in neo-Weberian theory of class is John **Goldthorpe**. Goldthorpe categorised **seven classes** based on occupation, with **three main classes** — service class ("white collar" professionals), intermediate class and working class.

An individual's **class position** is the **market position** he or she has in the **labour market**.

When the labour market **changes**, it may be necessary to **re-categorise** the classes.

Goldthorpe has been criticised for **neglecting** the particular position of **women** in the labour market — see **Arber, Dale** and **Gilbert (1986)**.

See p.58-59 for more on Goldthorpe's class scheme, and the NS-SEC classification which was developed from it.

Postmodern theory argues that Class is Dead

Postmodern theory says class is **no longer** of **central significance** in modern society. They **criticise** sociology for still focusing on **class** when other forms of **inequality** and **identity** are more relevant.

1) **Cultural differences** (values, lifestyles and beliefs) are what classify individuals to particular groups or strata in current society.

2) Postmodernists argue individuals are not governed by their economic position. Crucially, they say individuals can **place themselves** in groups or strata and move from one to another as their identity develops and changes.

3) **Pakulski and Waters (1996)** argue society has changed from an **economic class society** in 19th century, to a **hierarchical class society** in the first half of the 20th century, to a **status society** in the late 20th century.

In contrast, **Westergaard (1995)** criticises postmodern theory for ignoring the evidence that class still matters. He argues that as gaps between rich and poor are widening, class is **more** significant, not less, in the late 20th and 21st century.

Practice Questions

Q1 What are the two classes described by Marx?

Q2 What three types of power does Weber acknowledge?

Q3 What do postmodernists say about class?

Exam Questions

Q1 Identify and explain two ways in which the concept of class can be related to one or more of the following topics: families and households; health; education; work and leisure. (8 marks)

Q2 Assess the importance of class in British society from different sociological perspectives. (40 marks)

You should have guessed when there were no Marxists on the last page...

You knew deep inside it was too good to be true. Marx ignores the middle class, mainly because there wasn't really a middle class in the 1840s. Neo-Marxists acknowledge that society today is more complex. Weberians base everything on labour market position. And postmodernists pop up to say that class doesn't exist in a postmodern world, and that identities are all self-built anyway.

Differences in Opportunity

An individual's chance of experiencing good and bad sides of life are greatly influenced by the social groups they're born into. You'll see this referred to as life-chances. From a sociologist's perspective, the evidence shows we're not born equal.

The **Higher** an individual's **Social Class**, the **Better Chances** they have in life

This is almost **common knowledge** — but in sociology you have to give **evidence** to go along with common knowledge stuff.

1) Class affects an individual's chances from birth. The chances of a child dying before their first birthday are much higher if they're born into a lower social class.

Infant Mortality Rates in the UK (per 1000 live births)	1991	2001
Professional class	5.1	3.6
Unskilled Manual Class	8.2	7.2
Overall rate	5.3	4.6

Social Trends 33, (2003)

2) When a child goes to school, their chances of achieving good results are better if they're in a higher social class.

3) When they go on to work they're more likely to become unemployed if they're from a working class background — **Goldthorpe and Payne (1986)**.

% achieving 5 or more A-C GCSE grades	2002
Higher professional	77%
Routine workers	32%

Social Trends 34, (2004)

4) If they stay in work they're more likely to be paid less in a lower class occupation than in a middle class occupation.

5) An individual is more likely to suffer ill health and poor medical resources if they're working class. The **Black Report (1980)** and **Acheson Report (1998)** document this in detail.

Gross Weekly Incomes 2002	
Non-manual (men)	£608
Manual (men)	£366

Social Trends 33, references 2002 New Earnings Survey

6) Finally, social class affects how long a person lives.

Average Age at Death 1997-99	Men	Women
Professional class	78.5	82.8
Unskilled manual class	71.1	77.1
Overall	75.0	79.7

This is a synoptic unit, so remember to refer back to class differences in education and health, which you did for AS level..

There are **Health Inequalities** between **Women** and **Men**

1) Women made up 55% of the UK population in 2001 (the last census).

2) On average women live five years longer than men. In 2001 average age at death was 75 years for men and 80 years for women. In fact, **death rates** are higher for males than females in all age groups.

3) Men in the UK are more likely to **commit suicide** than women, again in all age groups. There's not yet been a great deal of sociological research into the causes of elevated male death rate and suicide rate — a little, but not much.

4) Women are more likely to be **diagnosed** with mental health problems. Some sociologists say this is because of more stressful lives, while others say it's to do with sexism within the medical profession.

In a 2000 survey of people aged 18-74, **20% of women** had enough **symptoms** in the week before the survey to be diagnosed as having a **neurotic disorder**. This was compared to **14% of men**.

Neurotic disorders = depression, anxiety, phobias, obsessive-compulsive disorder

(Office of National Statistics — Psychiatric Morbidity Among Adults Living in Private Households, 2000)

UK women experience **Inequalities** in **Life Chances**

1) Women **earn less** than men and are **less likely** to be in the **top jobs**. There's still a "glass ceiling". In sociology-speak, the labour market is "**vertically** segregated in terms of gender" (men on one level, women on another).

- In 1996, **23%** of board members of **British government bodies** were women.
- After the labour election win of 1997 there were many **new women MPs** (they were known at the time as "Blair's babes") but even with this increase only **18% of MPs** were women
- In 1994-5 **93%** of all **professors** in English universities were **men**.

(Office for National Statistics, 2000)

2) Some **occupations** are almost exclusively **female** — e.g. primary school teaching. There are **more women** than men in **clerical** jobs, in **retail**, and in **catering**. There are more **male** than female **building site foremen**. In sociology-speak, the labour market is "**horizontally** segregated in terms of gender" (men on one side and women on another, on the same level of the class hierarchy). Some of these "feminine" jobs may be lower paid than equivalent masculine jobs.

Differences in Opportunity

Ethnic Minorities are more likely to experience Discrimination and Inequality

1) **8%** of the current UK population belong to an **ethnic minority** — Social Trends 33, (2003).

2) People in households headed by someone from an **ethnic minority** are more likely to be at the **bottom** of the **income scale** than those where the head of household was **white** — Social trends 33, 2003.

3) **Bangladeshi** and **Pakistani** groups have the **highest unemployment** rates in the UK.

> In the UK in 2001-2002, **21%** of **Bangladeshis** were unemployed and **16%** of **Pakistanis**, compared with **4%** of the **white** population, **6%** of the **Chinese** population and **7%** of the **Indian** population.

It's important to distinguish between different ethnic minority groups.

(Annual Labour Force Survey, reported in Social trends 33, 2003)

4) **Bangladeshis**, **Pakistanis** and **Black Caribbeans** were **least likely** to be in the **highest socio-economic group**, (higher managers and professionals).

> In 2001-2002, **3%** of the **top social class** were **Bangladeshi**, **4%** were **Pakistani** and **5% Black Caribbean**, compared to **11% Chinese**, and **34% White** (made up of **8% White British**, **10% White Irish** and **16% Other White**)

(Annual Labour Force Survey, reported in Social trends 34, 2004)

5) People of **Bangladeshi**, **Black African** and **Other Black** origin were **most likely** to live in housing in the **social rented sector** (rented from the council and housing associations). Whites and Indians were most likely to own their home.

> In 2001, **48%** of **Bangladeshis**, **50%** of **Black Africans** and **50%** of **Other Black** were in social rented housing, compared to **8% Indian** and **17% White** British. **79%** of **Indians** and **71%** of **White British** were owner-occupiers.

(2001 census)

Important **public inquiries** have found evidence of **racism** in modern Britain, in many areas of life. The **Gifford Report (1989)** found evidence of **widespread racism** in the police force. The post-Brixton riot **Scarman Report (1981)** said Britain wasn't institutionally racist, but public policy often had **unintended consequences** that **disadvantaged ethnic minorities**. The **MacPherson Report (1999)** into the investigation of the Stephen Lawrence murder said that the police force was institutionally racist, and said that the recommendations of the Scarman Report had been ignored.

Both the Young and the Old face Inequality in Life Chances

1) Young people have **lower wages** than average — this is partly to be expected, as they lack job experience. Young people are more likely to be **unemployed** than the average.

2) Old people also have **low incomes**, because of **poor pension provision** and **ageism** in employment.

3) Britain has an ageing population. The number of people aged **65 and older** has increased by **51%** since **1961** — **Social Trends (2003)**. There are now more over 65s than under 16s. These social trends have led to a changing position for older people in society.

4) **Pressure groups** campaign for fairer treatment of older people. They have a powerful voice with politicians because they make up a large section of the voting public and a powerful voice with business and industry because they make up a large section of the **spending** public. There have been campaigns to stop **ageism** in the **workplace**, improve **pension** levels, and improve **care** and **housing** rights and resources.

Practice Questions

Q1 Define the term life-chances.
Q2 Give examples of how social class can affect opportunities open to an individual.
Q3 Give an example of social inequality affecting a) men and b) women.
Q4 Which ethnic groups are most likely to be unemployed?
Q5 Give an example of social inequality affecting young people.

Exam Question

Q1 "Structured inequalities affect the opportunities and experiences of every individual in the UK." Discuss with reference to one or more of the following topics: education, work and leisure, families and households, poverty and welfare. (40 marks)

See, it's all fair after all — women are paid less, but get to live longer...

If you're a stats geek, the Office of National Statistics website will ring your bell. They have huge mountains of statistics on just about every sociological factor you can think of. If stats aren't your thing, just learn the stats on these pages. You need some statistics to back up your argument in the exam — they don't give high marks for wild guesses and flights of fancy.

SECTION SIX — STRATIFICATION AND DIFFERENTIATION

Changes in the Class Structure

No system of social stratification is fixed and static. The British stratification system has undergone considerable change in the 20th century — alongside the changes in society. I sense you switching off again — stop it at once.

There's been a *Change* in *Work* patterns

1) Britain in the 20th century has seen a **decline in manual jobs** and an increase in non-manual jobs. The 1997 Labour Market Trends report shows that between 1983 and 1997, production jobs fell from 5,644,000 to 4,245,000.

2) Much of this trend is related to the increase in the service industries such as **leisure** and **entertainment**. The Welfare State also created a new sector of non-manual jobs. The **NHS** is the **largest employer** in **Europe**.

3) **Women** have become an **equal part** of the **workforce**. During the 20th century there's been a **dramatic increase** in the number of **women** who have **paid jobs**. Since 1971 it's gone up from 56% of women to 70% of women.

There have been changes in *Income* and *Wealth Distribution*

1) Statistics show that in the 20th century there was a steady pattern of both **income** and **wealth** being more **widely distributed** across the British population — until the 1980s when the trends were reversed.

2) There are still **big differences** in income in the UK, and the change in distribution has largely been from the upper class to the **middle classes**, not to the poorest.

3) Wealth is harder to measure (not all wealth has to be declared). Most wealth remains in the hands of a **minority**.

4) Despite increased wealth of the population, the **gap** between rich and poor remains.

The *Ruling Class* has *Changed* — opinions differ on just *How Much*

The New Right say that the ruling class has disintegrated.
Peter Saunders (1990) argues that the increase in the number of people **owning shares** in the UK has led to power being spread more widely. The small minority in power has been replaced with a **nation of stakeholders**.

Marxists insist the ruling class is alive and kicking.

1) **John Scott (1982, 1991)** agrees with Saunders that **more and more people own shares** in the UK but argues this hasn't led to a break-up of the ruling class. Most individuals own a **few** shares but hold **very little** real **power**.

2) Scott, and **Westergaard and Resler (1976)** say there's still a **power elite** who own **vast amounts** of **shares** and control business and the economy.

3) Scott says the **lifestyle** of the ruling class has changed — it's not all about "Hooray Henries" any more. However, changes in the lifestyle of the ruling class shouldn't be confused for a change in the **power** they hold. Wealth and power is still passed on through families — in 1990, 104 of the 200 richest families had inherited their wealth.

The *Middle Class* has *Grown*, but may be *Breaking Up* into *Several Classes*

1) The rise of the **professions** such as teaching, law and medicine have been cited by Functionalist and Weberian sociologists as evidence of an expanding middle class.

2) **Embourgeoisement** means working class people taking **middle class jobs** and **becoming middle class**. It was popular in sociology in the 1950s and 1960s to explain how the highest paid working class people became middle class in **lifestyle**, **wealth** and **values** as they became more affluent. This concept was used to predict a future where British society would be **largely middle class**. But reality wasn't quite so straightforward.

3) **Goldthorpe et al (1968)** tested the embourgeoisement thesis by interviewing car workers in Luton. They concluded that affluence had **not** made the workers middle class, and clear differences remained between them and the non-manual middle class workers — e.g. their attitudes to work and possibility of future promotion.

Some say the middle class is fragmenting into several middle classes with different life-chances and experiences.

1) **Goldthorpe** says there's an **Intermediate Class** of low grade non-manual workers who have little in common with middle class professionals. In terms of wages, perks, and relationship with employers, these groups are totally distinct.

2) Marxist **Harry Braverman (1974)** says many non-manual workers have been de-skilled by technology, so that they now have more in common with the working class in terms of job security and wealth. This is **proletarianisation**.

3) **Roberts et al (1977)** interviewed "middle class" workers about their view of their own class position and found wide variations in how groups saw themselves. They concluded the middle class is divided into smaller strata which have distinct values and positions in the structure of society — "the middle class are being splintered."

4) Influential sociologist **Giddens (1973)** disagrees — he says there's a **distinct middle class**. The middle class is distinct from the working class because its members can sell their **"brain power"** as well as, or **instead of**, their **labour power**.

Changes in the Class Structure

The 20th Century has Weakened and Divided the British Working Class

The decline in the **traditional working class** sectors of **manufacturing** and **heavy industry** in the 20th century has reduced the **size** of the British **working class**.

	1911	1971
manual work as % of employment	75%	49%

Routh (1981, 1987)

1) **Ralph Dahrendorf (1959)** argues that instead of uniting, the working class has disintegrated.

2) He said that the working class has been divided into groups of **skilled**, **semi-skilled** and **unskilled** workers, and that this is because of changes in technology.

3) Dahrendorf is criticised by **Penn (1985)**, whose research into cotton mills in Rochdale suggests that the working class has been divided into skilled, semi-skilled and unskilled since at least the **1850s**.

4) **Crewe (1983)** argues that the working class is splitting into groups with different concerns and interests, so it can no longer be considered a "real" class. He says that there's a "**new working class**" who live mainly in the South, work in the private sector and own their own homes. They have very different life experiences to the "old working class" who live mainly in the North, in council houses, and work in the public sector.

The idea that the working class is on its way out has been criticised, particularly by Marxist sociologists.

1) Marxist sociologists say that the working class can change its occupation and still be working class.

2) **Beynon (1992)** points out that the old working class jobs have been replaced by new occupations which are **equally badly paid** with poor conditions and rights — e.g. call centres, fast food outlets and hotels. Beynon says that **cooking burgers** is **manual, repetitive labour**, just like working on an assembly line in a factory.

3) Marxists argue what hasn't changed is the **status, rights** and **power** that go with the employment — the lack of these things is what makes it working class.

Remember the connection to **globalisation** (see glossary) — part of the reason that manufacturing working class jobs have vanished in the UK is because they've **moved abroad** to cheaper labour markets. There's an "**international division of labour**". Globally, the **working class** includes workers in **South East Asia** and **China** who have few rights and low pay.

Some Sociologists say there is an Underclass beyond the working class

The idea that the most **disadvantaged** groups in society are a **separate group** from the working class isn't **new**. Marx referred to the "lumpenproletariat" (beggars, pickpockets) and the "relative surplus" (people who aren't part of the regular labour market, but who do casual labour when needed). The idea of an underclass has gained support in the late 20th century.

1) The New Right see the underclass as dangerous to society. American sociologist **Charles Murray (1989)** defines the underclass by **behaviour** — **uneducated, delinquent** and **work-shy**.

2) **Runciman (1990)** defines the underclass as people who are **permanently dependent** on **welfare benefits**.

3) **Giddens (1973)** defines the underclass as those who are **most disadvantaged** in the job market — e.g. illegal immigrants. He says there's a **secondary job market** of **low paid** jobs with **low job security**, which are the best the underclass can get.

Practice Questions

Q1 Identify 2 long term trends which have affected the British class structure in the 20th century.

Q2 Explain Saunders' argument that the ruling class is no longer relevant in modern Britain.

Q3 Explain what sociologists mean by the terms embourgeoisement and proletarianisation.

Exam Questions

Q1 Examine the argument put forward by some sociologists that the working class has become so divided in the 20th century that it can no longer be considered a "real" class. (12 marks)

Q2 Evaluate the reasons put forward by sociologists for changes in the British class structure in the twentieth century. (40 marks)

Breaking up is so very hard to do...

There are a ridiculous number of sociologists on this page. I know it's a Sociology book, but still. I mean, for heaven's sake. It starts off OK until we reach Peter Saunders, and then they just start closing in on you. Scott starts agreeing and Goldthorpe starts testing and then Giddens disagrees and Penn criticises Dahrendorf... please, sociologists, just give it a rest. Seriously.

Social Mobility

Social mobility is all about how easy it is for people to change class. Like if you just go next door and start doing history.

Learn these **Definitions** of **Mobility**

Social mobility = the movement from one strata (class) to another.

Intra-generational mobility = social mobility of the same person within their **lifetime** — i.e. whether they stay in the same class **all their life**.

Inter-generational mobility = Social mobility **between generations** — i.e. whether a person stays in the same social class as their **parents**.

Absolute Mobility = how much social mobility there is in the society as a whole.

Relative Mobility = how much social mobility different social groups have relative to each other.

Upward mobility is fun.

One general rule to remember — the amount of **social mobility** is higher in societies where status is **achieved** than in societies where status is **ascribed** (given at birth). The amount of social mobility shows how **meritocratic** a society is. High mobility shows that people can **achieve** positions on **merit** regardless of the class they were born into.

The **First** major study of **Social Mobility** in Britain was by **Glass** in 1954

Glass (1954) compared social class of fathers and sons

Yes, that's a long time ago, but it's a classic study — and a springboard for all the research that's happened since.

David Glass used statistical data and analysis to compare the class of fathers and sons. He found there was a high level of social mobility — two thirds of sons were in a different social class from their father. This mobility was equally split — one third upward and one third downward.

But, the social mobility was mostly short-range. Most sons moved to the next class up or the next class down. (Glass categorised seven classes). The study also found that the upper class had fewer people moving in or out of it than the other classes.

Conclusion: The evidence was Britain was a society with unequal opportunities for individuals of all classes to reach the top.

The **Oxford Mobility Study** found **Higher** rates of **Social Mobility** in 1972

This study was conducted by **Goldthorpe et al** and used Goldthorpe's seven class scheme (see p.59). You'll see this referred to as the Oxford Study, the Goldthorpe Study or the Nuffield study. Whatever the name, it's the same study.

Goldthorpe (1980) also compared social class of fathers and sons

This study was done in 1972, but not published until 1980.

Results:	There were higher rates of social mobility than in 1949 — half of all sons were in a different social class from their fathers. More of this movement was to a **higher social class** than down to a **lower** one.
Conclusion:	Opportunities for working class individuals had improved in the second half of the 20th century. This has been used by Functionalist sociologists to show that Britain has become a more open and meritocratic society.
However:	Closer analysis showed that the chances of getting into the higher classes were much greater for those whose fathers were already there. There was some movement but relatively the upper classes were still better off.

A neat summary of the probabilities of upward mobility and downward mobility is given by **Kellner and Wilby (1980)**. The data revealed a **1:2:4** rule of "relative hope" — whatever the chance of a **working class** son being in the **professional class** as an adult, it was **twice** as much for an **intermediate class** son and four times as much for an **upper class** son. So, this study has also been used by sociologists to show Britain is an unfair society.

Upper class people tend to be **Born Upper Class**

There's a much greater chance of **higher class** individuals **staying** in that class than **working class** individuals **moving up**. The top classes in the UK remain very **static** — the majority of members come from families who have been in the upper class for **generations**. The elite recruit the sons of those already in the elite (elite self-recruitment).

1) **Stanworth and Giddens (1974)** found that of the top company positions in over four hundred British companies, only 1% were occupied by individuals with working class origins.

2) **Goldthorpe and Payne (1986)** did a follow-up to the Oxford study, looking at mobility rates during the **economic recession** of the 1970s. They concluded that mobility rates had **increased generally** but the chances of reaching **top classes** remained **unequal** in favour of those already there.

3) The **Essex study** of social mobility by **Marshall et al (1988)** looked at 1984 data and found that social mobility was increasing, but it was mainly short-range. Working class children are less likely to get top jobs. The **Essex study** also showed that working class people who got upper class jobs were less likely to retain them than upper class people.

Social Mobility

Other sociologists say the Social Mobility Data shows Britain is Meritocratic

There **aren't many** sociologists who interpret the data as evidence of **equality of opportunity** but there are some.

1) The main man is the New Right thinker, **Peter Saunders**. He uses the Essex study and The National Development Survey to conclude that the **opportunities** are there for social mobility but the **individual** has to get off their backside and take them.

2) Saunders argues the inequality that exists results from differences in the **talent** and **hard work** of the individual — not their class of origin.

> "Class destinations reflect **individual merit** much more than class background." — **Saunders (1996)**

3) Saunders has been **criticised** by many sociologists. His **methodology** is criticised — he **doesn't include** the **unemployed** and **part-time employees** in his analysis.

Remember labelling and education from the AS course.

4) Saunders' views have also been criticised because **class bias** at school could mean that school achievement reflects class background rather than ability. **Labelling** and **stereotypes** at school might discourage **working class** pupils from applying themselves to their studies.

Savage and Egerton (1997) analysed the **same** development survey as Saunders, but came to a very different conclusion. They found that those with the same ability didn't all have the same chances of ending up in the higher classes. Other factors such as **social networks**, **confidence** and **cultural capital** (see glossary) helped upper class children get to the top — e.g. they argue that educational qualifications and tests are based on middle and upper class culture and values. (This is covered in the AS course).

What about the girls — Women's Social Mobility wasn't studied until 1981

1) One of the biggest problems with the usefulness of the study of social mobility is that almost all major studies failed to take any account whatsoever of the class position of **girls** and **women**.

2) The first time women were included in a study was in 1981. **Heath (1981)** went back and looked at the statistics for 1971 and 1975 and compared **fathers'** and **daughters'** social class positions (still no mothers). He found that in classes one and two, **daughters** were much more likely to be **downwardly mobile** than sons.

3) **Goldthorpe and Payne (1986)** concluded that women's mobility rates varied according to which class they were in — just the **same as men**. They argue from this that the non-inclusion of women in previous studies didn't affect the overall results. Class overrode gender.

4) The **Essex study (1988)** looked at male and female mobility and found that women moved both up and down into the **routine non-manual** group — most routine non-manual work was done by women regardless of their class of origin.

5) **Savage and Egerton (1997)** looked at male and female mobility and found that class affected opportunity less for daughters than it did for sons. This may be because middle class sons can access an "**old boys' network**", or because of remaining sexism in traditional upper middle class jobs.

Feminist sociologists used to argue that as long as a woman's class is defined largely by the **male** she lives with (social class is defined by the occupation of the **Head of Household**, usually the **male** breadwinner), social mobility studies will reveal **very little** of significance about the impact of gender on social mobility. In **2000**, government statistics switched from a scheme that measured women by the **man's job** to a scheme which measured women by their **own job**. So, some **more useful studies** might come along soon — it'll be possible to see how a mother's occupational class affects her kids.

Practice Questions

Q1 Explain the different types of social mobility sociologists have studied.

Q2 What did the Oxford mobility study find out about social mobility?

Q3 What's meant by saying that the upper class is "static"?

Exam Question

Q1 Identify and explain two difficulties faced by sociologists when attempting to accurately measure social mobility. (8 marks)

Holy cats! It's the end of another book...

Famous people who studied Sociology include Martin Luther King, Ronald Reagan and Robin Williams. So if you want to follow in the footsteps of political leaders, or if you want to star in a sequel to "Mrs Doubtfire", then you've come to the right place. You just need to pass those all important exams — and that means revising (and turning up on time with a pen).

Do Well in Your Exam

These two pages are all about how to do well in your final exams.

These pages describe what the AQA Sociology exam papers have been like for the past few years. We can't predict exactly what new exam papers will be like though — there may be a few changes. So it's important that when you take the exams, you **read the instructions and questions really carefully**. Don't assume they'll always follow the same pattern.

The A2 Exam is split into *Three Units* — *units 4, 5 and 6*

The A2 exam is split into **three units**, and each of these units is tested by one **1.5 hour exam**.

You'll have to answer **data response questions** (where you're asked questions about sources) and **essay questions**.

Unit 4 has three core areas — 'Power and Politics', 'Religion' and 'World Sociology'

1) You only have to answer questions on **one** of these topics. You might decide to revise more than one, so you can choose the best questions on the day. Knowing about more than one of these topics might also help you answer the synoptic questions in Unit 6.

2) Each topic usually has a compulsory **data response question** divided into **two** subparts — (a) and (b). These questions are sometimes broken down into further subparts — (i) and (ii).

3) There's also an **essay question worth 40 marks** (there's usually a **choice** of two essay questions for each topic).

Unit 5 is the Sociological Theory and Methods unit

1) There's usually **one compulsory data response question**, and a long **essay question**.

2) The **data response** question is usually divided into four **subparts** (which may be divided into further subparts). You have to answer questions specifically about the items (sources), and some more general questions. This part of the paper is worth **20 marks** altogether.

3) The **essay question** is worth **40 marks**. You usually get a choice of two essay questions.

Unit 6 has a choice of two topics — 'Crime and Deviance' or 'Stratification and Differentiation'

1) Whichever topic you choose, there's a **compulsory three-part question** worth a **total of 60 marks** (some of these parts may be broken down into further subparts).

2) This unit is the **Synoptic Paper**, which means you need to use your knowledge from the **whole course, including your AS work**. You have to make **references** to and **links** with **other topics** (like 'Education and Stratification', 'Poverty and Crime') and with sociological **theories** and **methods**.

3) Each part of the question **tells you specifically** what kind of **synoptic links** it expects you to make.

4) This is the **only** unit which is tested synoptically — don't overlook it when you do your revision. The buzz word is **connections**. The examiners want you to demonstrate an understanding of how sociological issues and themes **overlap** and **interlink**, as they do in real life.

You Get Marks For...

AO just means 'Assessment Objective'

You Get Marks for AO1 — *Knowledge and Understanding* and AO2 — *Identification, Analysis, Interpretation and Evaluation*

1) In the A2 exam, more of the marks are for AO2 skills than they were at AS level.

2) This is significant. You must be able to draw on a wide range of studies and theories and **analyse** them in detail. However much knowledge you display, if you don't **analyse** and **evaluate** it you won't get high marks. Each year, the examiners' report complains that people chuck down **buckets of knowledge** without really **answering** the question.

3) So, make sure you do **exactly what the question says**. For example, if it says "**evaluate**" a theory, then **evaluate** it — give **strengths** and **weaknesses** and say why the theory might not work. Don't just outline the theory. If it says "how does this theory help us understand today's society?" then you need to do **more** than **describe** the theory — you need to say how it is or isn't relevant to specific features of society today.

4) Remember — A2 is not just studying new and different topics from AS, but studying topics in **more depth**. Examiners want to see:

- More evidence of **critical evaluation** and **interpretation**.
- More reflective, **critical understanding** of sociological **theory** and **method**.

Do Well in Your Exam

Take a concept and *Make It Work* for you

A way to build up those AO2 marks is to master the art of **writing about sociological concepts**.
There are key concepts in every topic — here's how to **wring the marks out of them**.

1) **Define** the concept.
2) Give **examples** of it in practice.
3) Present **different viewpoints** on the same concept.
4) Present **evidence** for each viewpoint.

And whatever you write, make sure it's 100% relevant to the question.

Use what you learnt in your *AS Level*

Don't make the mistake of **forgetting** all the Sociology you learnt to get your stunning AS grade. The key research and theories will be relevant to these exam questions, too — especially unit 6, the synoptic unit. Use it, don't lose it.

Oh... and don't forget **the basics**.

The AQA examiners really care about stuff like being able to read your handwriting — they're always going on about it in their examiners' reports.

- Write as **neatly** as you can.
- Use good **grammar** and **punctuation**.
- Check your **spelling** — especially of words to do with sociology.
- Make sure you **answer the question**.

Here's an *Example Essay* to show you what to aim for:

> **Assess the view that religion is in decline in the UK.** (40 marks)

Mention relevant studies.

Bryan Wilson (1966) describes a process of secularisation. This is a decline in the significance of religious belief, religious institutions and religious practice in society. Evidence about the influence of religion in society is often open to different interpretations; it is difficult to prove definitively that religion is in decline.

Define the key term or idea that the question asks you about.

In the 2001 census, 72% of the people in the UK identified themselves as Christian. However, these 72% who identify themselves as Christian do not necessarily hold strong religious beliefs. Some may have been brought up nominally Christian, but have minimal belief in God or the teachings of Christianity.

Evaluate how reliable data is — don't just take it at face value.

Church attendance figures are often used to support the view that religion is in decline — the percentage of adults who go to church has fallen from 10% to 7% over the last 20 years. This is a questionable method of judging the extent of secularisation though, as it only deals with religious practice, not religious belief. It's possible to attend church without having faith, just for the social networking aspects, as Herberg suggested. On the other hand, it is possible to believe strongly in God, but never go to church. Grace Davie (1995) called the first situation "belonging without believing" and the second situation "believing without belonging". Davie claimed that belonging to a church and believing in religion are getting more and more separated.

Have separate paragraphs about different aspects of a topic.

Some argue that religious institutions have lost influence in wider society. Wilson argues that religion is only involved in symbolic rituals, "hatching, matching and dispatching", and doesn't have relevance to everyday life.

Steve Bruce (1995) said that the Church became less important to people as its functions were taken over by other, secular institutions. For example, the Church used to have a strong role in education and welfare — roles which are now primarily filled by secular, state organisations. On the other hand, Parsons claims that even though the Church no longer has all the functions it had back in the middle ages, religion can still have an influence on people's everyday lives.

Discuss contrasting viewpoints.

There has been a trend towards religious pluralism (a greater variety of religions practised in British society). This is partly because of the immigration of ethnic minorities, and partly because of new religious movements (NRMs).

Immigrant groups often have a higher level of religiosity than the settled population. Religion contributes to a sense of community and ethnic identity. Davie claimed that identification with a religion was important to South Asian immigrants because it gave a strong sense of cultural identity. Bruce refers to cultural transition — when South Asian immigrants came to the UK, they quickly set up religious institutions to act as a support structure for the immigrant community.

Bring in relevant examples.

Religious pluralism has also resulted from the growth of new religious movements (NRMs) since the 1960s. A large variety of groups and beliefs have been labelled NRMs, from the Moonies to Reiki healers. Many sociologists use the growth of NRMs as evidence to argue against secularisation. Sociologists have claimed that the conditions of modernity and postmodernity create insecurity and alienation, and that the growth of NRMs is a response to this. However, it is not easy to use the rise in NRMs as evidence against secularisation. Some NRMs are very vague in their beliefs, and may not count as religions at all.

Explain your opinion on the topic, based on the evidence in the essay.

In conclusion, it is difficult to accurately measure whether religion is declining. Personal belief is a complex topic; for example even if a person says they are Christian, they may not attend Church or believe strongly in God. The rise of NRMs since the 1960s suggests that many people do want some element of spirituality in their lives, but it is arguable whether this is the equivalent of a traditional religion.

Glossary

bourgeoisie Marxist term for the capitalist ruling class. They own the means of production (e.g. factories, equipment, raw materials).

capitalism An economic system based on private ownership of the means of production, distribution and exchange of commodities. In the capitalist system, labour itself becomes a commodity which employers buy for wages. Capitalism is associated with free trade and individual enterprise. It started in Europe and the US and has spread to become the dominant economic philosophy in most countries.

civil disobedience Protest action that breaks laws.

class A way of stratifying society, on the basis of people's social and economic status. Class is hierarchical — some classes are more privileged than others. The "class system" is criticised by Marxists.

classical liberalism The view that the market should be free, with minimum state intervention, and that individuals should take responsibility for themselves.

Communism A system of government which is theoretically based on a classless society and where private ownership has been abolished. It is influenced by the ideas of Marx and Engels. During the Cold War, there was conflict between capitalist Western countries and Communist countries like the USSR and China. With the end of the Cold War and the break up of the USSR, many formerly Communist countries have moved towards adopting capitalism. To some extent, this has discredited Communism as a viable political philosophy.

conformity Adherence to the norms and values of society. The opposite of deviance.

consensus Fundamental agreement within a society about that society's basic values. Functionalist theory suggests that, as a result of socialisation, the people in a society all share the same norms and values and this contributes to consensus.

correlation A measure of how closely two variables are related.

cultural capital The cultural skills and knowledge which children learn from their parents. Bourdieu claimed that upper and middle class children are more likely to have cultural capital than working class children and that this puts them at an advantage educationally.

cultural deprivation theory This theory claims that educational achievement and health vary according to social class because some classes lack the cultural values and knowledge which promote a healthy lifestyle and educational achievement.

culture The "way of life" of a society or group. Culture is made up of things such as language, customs, knowledge, norms and values. It is passed on by socialisation.

dependency theory A development theory which blames underdevelopment on colonialism.

desacrilisation Religious and spiritual beliefs ceasing to have a place in society.

deviance Something that goes against society's norms and values. Deviant behaviour is behaviour that society doesn't approve of.

discourse Any kind of discussion or communication (either written or spoken) about a subject. Foucault said that discourse was the rules and framework for how a topic can be discussed.

ethnocentric Centred around the values and interests of one particular ethnic group.

ethnography Research which studies the culture and way of life of a community. It is usually done by observation, and may also use interviews and case studies. Ethnography looks at social relationships, organisations, customs and practices. It is an Interactionist approach to sociological study and so produces qualitative data.

false consciousness Marxism says that workers are in a state of false consciousness about their place in society. They have learnt values and beliefs that support the interests of the ruling class (through their education, the media and religion), and this prevents them from realising how unfair capitalist society is.

false needs Things people think they need but which don't really satisfy them. Marxists say these false needs have been created by a capitalist culture which encourages consumerism.

falsification Trying to prove a hypothesis wrong.

feminism A broad movement which believes that social organisations and culture have been dominated by men to the exclusion of women. Feminists claim that this has devalued and disadvantaged women into a marginalised status. There are many varieties of feminism, e.g. liberal feminism, Marxist feminism, radical feminism and black feminism.

free market an economic system that lets supply and demand control prices, wages etc. rather than the government.

Functionalism An important sociological perspective about how society works, founded by Durkheim. Functionalists believe that society is made up of a number of institutions, each of which has a useful function and helps society to run smoothly, e.g. the family, the education system, religion. These institutions work in harmony because they have agreed norms and values, and this is essential for society to survive. Functionalists say that individuals internalise these norms and values (socialisation). Another term for Functionalism is "Consensus Structuralism". So now you know.

gender Sociologists say that gender (femininity and masculinity) is a social construction. Being male or female is the biological sex you're born with, while masculinity and femininity are identities you're socialised into.

globalisation The breaking down of traditional national boundaries as globally people become more interconnected. This happens due to factors such as the growth of multinational companies, improvements in communications and technology, increased migration of people between societies, and the global marketing of cultural products.

Hawthorne Effect When participants are aware they are taking part in an experiment, it often affects their behaviour. This is known as the Hawthorne Effect.

hegemony The domination of one group of people over others, or of one set of ideas and values over others. Law, religion, media, art science and literature may all be used to make the dominant group or values legitimate and to discredit the alternatives.

hierarchy A system which ranks people according to status. Any system where you have a boss in charge of people is a hierarchy.

hypothetico-deductive model Research favoured by positivist sociologists which is similar to the approach used in natural sciences. It involves using an experiment to test a hypothesis and then using the results to confirm, modify or reject the hypothesis.

identity An individual's sense of self. This can be influenced by social factors such as class, gender, religion and ethnicity.

ideological state apparatus Institutions like the media, schools, Church and family which can spread the ideology of the state.

ideology A set of ideas and beliefs about the way things should be — often politically motivated.

individualist welfare Welfare system with selective, means-tested benefits.

infrastructure In Marxist theory, the infrastructure is the economic base of society (e.g. labour and manufacturing).

institutional racism When the policies, attitudes and actions of an institution discriminate against ethnic minorities — sometimes unintentionally.

institutions of society Things like the family, the Church, the education system, the health care system.

Interactionism A sociological approach which focuses on the actions and thoughts of individuals. Society is viewed as the product of interaction between individuals. "Interactionism", "Interpretivism" and "Social Action theory" are pretty much the same thing — so don't get confused if you see these other terms being used.

labelling theory This theory says that the labels given to someone affect their behaviour, e.g. someone who is labelled a criminal is more likely to commit criminal acts. Labels also affect how other people treat someone, e.g. teachers might treat a child labelled a "troublemaker" more strictly.

LEDC Less Economically Developed Country.

Glossary

Left Realism Sociological viewpoint which developed from Marxism. The approach focuses on working within the capitalist framework and aims to direct social policy to help the poor.

Marxism A theory and political ideology based on the views of Karl Marx (1818-1883). Marxists are opposed to capitalism, which they believe is based on the exploitation of the working class (proletariat) by the owning class (bourgeoisie). Original Marxist ideas have been developed and adapted by **neo-Marxists**. Some states have been run politically along Marxist lines, e.g. Cuba under Castro.

mass media Ways of communicating with large numbers of people, e.g. newspapers, TV, magazines, radio, Internet.

master status a quality in an individual that comes to dominate the way that they are treated or viewed, to the extent that all their other qualities are disregarded. This quality then takes on the status of a label. E.g. if someone with mental health problems is given the often negative label "mentally ill", and then finds that all their other qualities are then ignored, the label "mentally ill" has master status.

MEDC More Economically Developed Country.

media text Any piece of media — e.g. a book, a TV programme, an advert.

meritocracy A system where the best (most talented and hard-working) people rise to the top.

metanarrative An over-arching, all-encompassing story which gives meaning to history and events.

modernism View of society that tries to come up with big theories to explain all of society (metanarratives). Modernists try to investigate society scientifically.

moral panic A fear of a moral crisis in society. The mass media have a big role in starting moral panics in modern society.

neo-Marxism In the 20th century, some of Marx's followers revised and adapted his ideas to make them more relevant to modern society. Neo-Marxists often stress the importance of culture in sustaining capitalism, e.g. through the hegemony of capitalist ideas. Neo-Marxists include Gramsci, Althusser and Stuart Hall.

norm A social rule about what is correct and appropriate behaviour within a particular culture, e.g. queuing in a shop.

patriarchy A society where men are dominant. Feminists often describe male-dominated societies and institutions as "patriarchal".

Physical Quality of Life Index (PQLI) A development index that measures infant mortality, literacy and life expectancy.

pluralism The belief that society is diverse and reflects the needs and views of everyone via democracy and the free market.

positivism A theoretical point of view which concentrates on social facts, scientific method and quantitative data (facts and figures). The positivist view is that human behaviour is determined by external social factors, and so is outside the control of the individuals in society.

post-Fordism Theory that work now tends to be more flexible and less repetitive than it was at the height of Fordism. It involves computer technology, multi-skilled workers, a less strict hierarchy, new organisation of workers and products made for quality rather than quantity.

postmodernism Theory which says there is no one objective truth or reality that everyone experiences. Postmodernism rejects the ideas of modernism, such as positivism and metanarratives.

postmodernity The world after the modern age — with flexible working, individual responsibility and people constructing their own identity.

poststructuralism The idea that there are no fixed meanings, and that people are controlled by language and signs.

qualitative methods of research Methods like unstructured interviews and participant observation that give results which tell a story about individuals' lives.

quantitative methods of research Methods like surveys and structured interviews that give results you can easily put into a graph or table.

reliability Data is reliable if other sociologists using the same methods on the same group collect the same data. Quantitative data is usually the most reliable.

representative democracy Rule by the people, via voting in elections for representatives (e.g. MPs).

sanctions Rewards and punishments that reinforce social norms.

secularisation When religion loses its influence in society.

social construct An idea or belief that's created in society, and doesn't come from a scientific fact.

Social Democrats People who think the state should redistribute wealth, and that there should be a strong Welfare State paid for out of taxes. Social democrats believe in social equality.

social policy Government decisions which affect society, e.g. raising taxes, changing the benefits system, privatisation.

socialisation Passing on cultural values and norms from one generation to the next, so that they become internalised, i.e. part of everyone's way of thinking.

stereotype A generalisation about a social group — often inaccurate and insulting.

stratification The way society is divided up into layers or classes.

stratified sample A sample with the same proportions of gender, class, age etc. as the population you're studying.

subculture A group who share values and norms which are different from the mainstream culture.

superstructure In Marxist theory, the superstructure is the institutions in a society which aren't economic (such as legal, political, cultural and religious institutions) and the beliefs and values which these institutions propagate. It has a role in maintaining and sustaining the economic infrastructure.

symbolic communities Communities connected to each other through leisure or culture.

symbolic consumption Buying things that define who you are, e.g. a particular brand of clothing.

third way politics A political viewpoint that combines elements of right wing self-sufficiency and left wing social democracy.

triangulation Combining different research methods and data to get the best results.

underclass A social group at the bottom of the social hierarchy. New Right sociologists think they're lazy and dependent on welfare. Left wing sociologists think they're disadvantaged by the welfare system.

validity Data is valid if it gives an accurate picture of what's being measured.

value free research Research that isn't biased, and isn't influenced by the researcher's beliefs.

values A general belief in a society about what is important or what is right and wrong, e.g. freedom of speech is a value of Western society.

victim survey Survey asking if respondents have been victims of crime.

vocational education Education that provides the skills needed for a particular job.

Weber (1864-1920) Influential, early sociologist. Weber argued that the better a person's market situation, the better their life-chances, wealth and status would be. He also suggested that, as societies developed, secularisation would follow as people came to believe more in science. Weberians are followers of Weber's work and ideas.

welfare pluralism Mixture of state, private, voluntary and informal welfare provision.

World Systems theory Development theory which looks at the world as a single economic system where some countries have a lot of power and others don't have power.

References

These are details of studies which are discussed in the Revision Guide.

Abbott, P. and Wallace, C. (1990) *An Introduction to Sociology: Feminist Perspectives* (London: Routledge)

Acheson Report (1998) *Independent Inquiry into Inequalities in Health*, Chairman Sir Donald Acheson (London: Stationery Office)

Adamson, P. (1986) 'The Rich, the Poor, the Pregnant' (*New Internationalist* Issue 270)

Akers, R.L. (1967) 'Problems in the sociology of deviance: Social definitions and behavior' (*Social Forces* 46)

Althusser, L. (1969) *Lenin and Philosophy and Other Essays* (New York: Monthly Review Press)

Arber, S., Dale, A. and Gilbert, N. (1986) 'The limitations of existing social class of women' in A. Jacoby (ed.) *The measurement of Social Class* (Guilford: Social Research Association)

Atkinson, J. M. (1978) *Discovering Suicide* (London: Macmillan)

Baechler, J. (1979) *Suicides* (Oxford: Blackwell)

Barker, E. (1984) *The Making of a Moonie* (Oxford: Blackwell)

Baudrillard, J. (1983) *Simulations* (New York: Semiotext)

Bauman, Z. (1990) *Thinking Sociologically* (Oxford: Blackwell)

de Beauvoir, S. (1953) *The Second Sex* (London: Jonathan Cape)

Becker, H. S. (1963) *Outsiders: Studies in the Sociology of Deviance* (New York: The Free Press)

Becker, H.S. (1970) *Sociological Work* (New Brunswick: Transaction)

Bellah, R. (1967) 'Civil Religion in America' (*Daedalus* 96 1-21)

Berger, P. and Luckman, T. (1971) *The social construction of reality — a treatise on the sociology of knowledge* (Harmondsworth: Penguin)

Berthoud, R. (1997) 'Income and Standards of living' in Modood et al. *Ethnic Minorities in Britain: Diversity and Disadvantage* (London: PSI)

Beynon, H. (1992) 'The end of the Industrial Worker' in Abercrombie, N. and Warde, A. (eds.) *Social Change in Contemporary Britain* (Cambridge: Polity Press)

Black Report (1980) *Inequalities in health: report of a research working group* (London: DHSS)

Bonger, W.A. (1916) *Criminality and economic conditions* (Boston: Little, Brown)

Bordua, D. (1962) 'Some Comments on Theories of Group Delinquency' (*Sociological Inquiry* 32)

Boserup, E. (1965) *The Conditions of Agricultural Growth* (Chicago: Aldine)

Bourdieu, P. (1984) *Distinction: A Social Critique of the Judgement of Taste* (Cambridge, Massachusetts: Harvard University Press)

Bourdieu, P. (1986) 'The Forms of Capital' in Richardson, J. (ed.) *Handbook of Theory and Research for the Sociology of Education* (New York: Greenwood Press)

Braverman, H. (1974) *Labour and Monopoly Capital* (New York & London: Monthly Review Press)

Brown, P. and Lauder, H. (1997) 'Education, Globalization, and Economic Development' in Halsey, A.H., Lauder, H., Brown, P. and Wells, A.S. (eds.) *Education, Culture, Economy, Society* (Oxford: Oxford University Press)

Bruce, S. (1995) *Religion in Modern Britain* (Oxford: OUP)

Bruce, S. (2002) *God is Dead: Secularization in the West* (Oxford: Blackwell)

Butler, D. and Kavanagh, D. (1985) *The British General Election of 1983* (London: MacMillan)

Campbell, A. (1981) *Delinquent Girls* (Oxford: Blackwell)

Carnap, R. (1936) 'Testability and Meaning' (*Philosophy of Science* 3)

Carnap, R. (1966) *The Philosophy of Science* (New York: Basic Books)

Carnell, B. (2000) 'Paul Ehrlich' (www.overpopulation.com)

Chambliss, W.J. (1978) *On the Take: From Petty Crooks to Presidents* (Bloomington, Indiana: Indiana University Press)

Chambliss, W.J. and Mankoff, M. (1976) *Whose Law? What Order?* (New York: Wiley & Sons)

Cicourel, A.V. (1968) *The Social Organisation of Juvenile Justice* (New York: John Wiley)

Cloward, R. and Ohlin, L. (1960) *Delinquency and Opportunity: A Theory of Delinquent Gangs.* (Glencoe, Illinois: Free Press)

Cohen, A. F. S. (1955) *Delinquent Boys* (Glencoe, Illinois: The Free Press)

Cohen, A. K. (1966) *Deviance and Control* (Englewood Cliffs, New Jersey: Prentice-Hall)

Cohen, S. (ed.) (1971) *Images of Deviance* (London: Penguin)

Cohen, S. (1972) *Folk Devils and Moral Panics* (London: Paladin)

Crewe, I. (1983) 'The disturbing truth behind Labour's rout' (*The Guardian*, 13 June)

Crewe, I. (1985) 'Can Labour rise again?' (*Social Studies Review* Sept.)

Crewe, I. (1987) 'A new class of politics' (*The Guardian*, 16 June)

Dahl, R.A. (1961) *Who Governs?* (New Haven: Yale University Press)

Dahrendorf, R. (1959) *Class and Class Conflict in an Industrial Society* (London: Routledge & Kegan Paul)

Dale, A., Gilbert, G.N. and Arber, S. (1985) 'Integrating Women into Class Theory' (*Sociology*, 19)

Davie, G. (1994) *Religion in Britain since 1945. Believing without Belonging* (Oxford: Blackwell)

Davie, G. (2000) *Religion in Modern Europe. A Memory Mutates* (Oxford: OUP)

Davis, K. and Moore, W.E. (1945) 'Some Principles of Stratification' (*American Sociological Review* 10, 242-249)

Devine, F. (1992) *Affluent Workers Revisited* (Edinburgh: Edinburgh University Press)

Douglas, J.D. (1967) *The Social Meanings of Suicide* (Princeton, New Jersey: Princeton University Press)

Downes, D. and Rock, P. (1988) *Understanding Deviance: a guide to the sociology of crime and rule-breaking* 2nd edition (Oxford: Oxford University Press)

Durkheim, E. (1897 translated 1951) *Suicide: A Study in Sociology* (London: Routledge)

Edgell, S. (1993) *Class* (London: Routledge)

Ehrlich, P. R. (1968) *The Population Bomb* (New York: Ballantine Books)

Eisenstadt, S.N. (1967) 'The Protestant Ethic Thesis' (*Diogenes* 59)

Feyerabend, P. (1975) *Against Method* (London: Verso)

Field, F. (1989) *Losing Out: The Emergence of Britain's Underclass* (Oxford: Blackwell)

Field, F. (1996) *Stakeholder Welfare* (Institute of Economic Affairs)

Fielding, N. (1981) *The National Front* (London: Routledge & Kegan Paul)

Firestone, S. (1971) *The Dialectic of Sex* (London: Cape)

Frank, A.G. (1967) *Capitalism and Underdevelopment in Latin America* (New York: Monthly Review Press)

Frank, A.G. (1971) *Sociology of Development and Underdevelopment of Sociology* (London: Pluto Press)

Friedman, M. (1962) *Capitalism and Freedom* (Chicago: Chicago University Press)

Fröbel, F., Heinrichs, J. and Kreye, O. (1980) *The New International Division of Labour* (Cambridge: CUP)

Fulcher, J. and Scott, J. (1999) *Sociology* (Oxford: OUP)

Fuller, M. (1980) 'Black Girls in a London Comprehensive School' in Deem, R. (ed.) *Schooling for Women's Work* (London: Routledge & Kegan Paul)

Gerth, H. and Mills, C. (eds.) (1948) *From Max Weber, Essays in Sociology* (London: Routledge & Kegal Paul)

George, V. and Page, R. (eds.) *Thinkers on Modern Welfare* (London: Hutchinson)

Gibbs, J. and Martin, W.T. (1964) *Status Integration and Suicide* (Eugene, Oregon: University of Oregon Press)

Giddens, A. (1973) *The Class Structure of the Advanced Societies* (London: Hutchinson)

Giddens, A. (1984) *The Constitutions of Society* (Cambridge: Polity Press)

Giddens, A. (1987) *Social Theory and Modern Sociology* (Cambridge: Polity Press)

Giddens, A. (1990) *The Consequences of Modernity* (Cambridge: Polity Press)

Giddens, A. (1991) *Modernity and Self-Identity: Self and Society in the Late Modern Age* (Cambridge: Polity Press)

Giddens, A. (1998) *The Third Way — the Renewal of Social Democracy* (Cambridge: Polity Press)

Giddens, A. (2001) *Sociology* 4th edition (Cambridge: Polity Press)

Gifford, Lord (1986) *The Broadwater Farm Inquiry* (London: Karia)

Gifford, Lord (1989) *Loosen the Shackles: first report of the Liverpool 8 inquiry into race relations in Liverpool* (London: Karia).

References

Gilroy, P. (1987) 'The Myth of Black Criminality' in Scraton, P. (ed.) *Law, Order and the Authoritarian State* (Milton Keynes: Open University Press)

Glass, D. V. and Hall, J. R. (1954) 'Social mobility in Great Britain: a study of inter-generation changes in status' in Glass (ed.) *Social Mobility in Britain* (London: Routledge & Kegan Paul)

Glock, C.Y. and Bellah, R.N. (eds.) (1976) *The New Religious Consciousness* (Berkeley, CA: University of California Press)

Glock, C.Y. and Stark, R. (1965) *Religion and Society in Tension* (Chicago: Rand McNally)

Goffman, E. (1961) *Asylums* (Harmondsworth: Penguin)

Goldthorpe, J.H. (1980) *Social Mobility and Class Structure in Modern Britain* (Oxford: Clarendon Press)

Goldthorpe, J.H., Lockwood, D., Bechhofer, F., and Platt, J. (1968) *The Affluent Worker in the Class Structure* (Cambridge: CUP)

Goldthorpe and Payne (1986) 'On the Class Mobility of Women' (*Sociology* vol. 20)

Goldthorpe and Payne (1986) 'Trends in intergenerational mobility in England and Wales 1979-1983' (*Sociology* vol. 20)

Gordon (1976) 'Class and the economics of crime' in Chambliss, W.J. and Mankoff, M. (1976) *Whose Law? What Order?* (New York: Wiley & Sons)

Gouldner, A. (1973) *For Sociology: Renewal and Critique in Sociology Today* (New York: Basic Books)

Gramsci, G. (1971) *Selections from the Prison Notebooks* (London: Lawrence and Wishart)

Grant, W. and Marsh, D. (1977) *The Confederation of British Industry* (London: Hodder & Stoughton)

Habermas, J. (1987) *The Theory of Communicative Action*, vol.2 (Boston: Beacon Press)

Halbwachs, M. (1930) *Les Causes du Suicide* (Paris: Alcan)

Halevy, E. (1927) *A History of the English People in 1815* (London: Unwin)

Hall, S. (1995) 'Negotiating Caribbean Identities' (*New Left Review*, 209)

Hall, S., Critcher, C., Jefferson, T., Clarke, J. and Roberts, B. (1978) *Policing the Crisis* (London: Macmillan)

Hallsworth, S. (1994) 'Understanding New Social Movements' (*Sociology Review*, Vol. 4 no. 1)

Halsey, A. H., Heath, A. F., and Ridge, J. M. (1980) *Origins and Destinations* (Oxford: Clarendon)

Harrison (1990) *Inside the Third World: The Anatomy of Poverty* 2nd edition (Harmondsworth: Penguin)

Hayek, F. von (1944) *The Road to Serfdom* (Chicago: University of Chicago Press)

Hayter, T. (1971) *Aid as Imperialism* (Harmondsworth: Penguin)

Hayter, T. (1981) *The Creation of World Poverty* (London: Pluto Press)

Hayter, T. (1989) *Exploited Earth: Britain's Aid and the Environment* (London: Earthscan)

Heath, A. F. (1981) *Social Mobility* (Glasgow: Fontana)

Hebdige, D. (1979) *Subculture: The Meaning of Style* (London: Routledge)

Heelas, P. (1996) *The New Age Movement* (Oxford: Blackwell)

Heidensohn, F. (1986) *Women and Crime* (London: Macmillan)

Hempel, C. (1966) *Philosophy of Natural Science* (Englewood Cliffs, New Jersey: Prentice Hall)

Herberg, W. (1956) *Protestant – Catholic – Jew* (New York: Doubleday)

Hewitt, C.J. (1974) 'Elites and the distribution of power in British society' in Stanworth, P. and Giddens, A. (eds.) *Elites and Power in British Society* (Cambridge: CUP)

Hoselitz, B.F. (1964) *Sociological Aspects of Economic Growth* (Glencoe: The Free Press)

Humphreys, L. (1970) *Tearoom Trade: Impersonal Sex in Public Places* (Chicago: Aldine Atherton)

Hutton, W. (1995) *The State we're in: Why Britain is in Crisis and how to Overcome it* (London: Vintage)

Hutton, W. (1997) 'Spend to save welfare and to make work' (*The Observer* 21st September)

Hyman, H. H. (1967) 'The Value Systems of Different Classes' in Bendix, R. and Lipset, S.M. (eds.) *Class, Status and Power* (London: Routledge & Kegan Paul)

Jacques, M. and Hall, S. (1997) 'Cultural Revolution' (*New Statesman* vol. 10, Dec 5th)

Johal (1998) 'Brimful of Brasia' (*Sociology Review*, 8)

Kellner, P. and Wilby, P. (1980) 'The 1: 2: 4 rule of class in Britain' (*Sunday Times* 13th January)

Kerr, C., Dunlop, J., Harbison, F. and Mayers, C. (1962) *Industrialism and Industrial Man* (London: Heinemann)

Kuhn, T.S. (1962) *The Structure of Scientific Revolutions* (Chicago: University of Chicago Press)

Labov, W. (1973) "The logic of non-standard English" in Keddie, N. (ed) *Tinker, Tailor – The Myth of Cultural Deprivation.* (Harmondsworth: Penguin)

Lemert, E. (1951) *Social Pathology* (New York: McGraw Hill)

Luckmann, T. (1967) *The Invisible Religion* (New York: Macmillan)

Lukes, S. (1974) *Power: a Radical View* (London: Macmillan)

Lupton, T. and Wilson, C.S (1973) 'The Social Background and connections of top decision makers' in Urry and Wakeford (eds.) *Power in Britain, sociological readings* (London: Heinemann)

Lyotard, J.F. (1984) *The Postmodern Condition* (Manchester: Manchester University Press)

MacPherson of Cluny, Sir William (1999) *The Stephen Lawrence Inquiry: Report on an Inquiry by Sir William MacPherson of Cluny* (London: The Stationery Office)

Mack, J. and Lansley, S. (1985) *Poor Britain* (London: Allen & Unwin)

Maduro, O. (1982) *Religion and Social Conflicts* (Maryknoll, New York: Orbis Books)

Malinowski, B. (1954) *Magic, Science, Religion and Other Essays* (New York: Anchor Books)

Malthus, T. (1798) *An Essay on the Principle of Population* (London)

Marcuse, H. (1964) *One Dimensional Man* (London: Routledge & Kegan Paul)

Marcuse, H. (1969) *An Essay on Liberation* (Boston: Beacon Press)

Marsh, D. and Locksley, G. (1983) 'Labour: the Dominant Force in British Politics?' in D. March (ed.) (1983) *Pressure Politics: interest groups in Britain* (London: Junction Books)

Marsh, I. (1986) *Sociology In Focus: Crime* (London: Longman)

Marshall, G., Newby, H., Rose, D. and Vogler, C. (1988) *Social Class in Modern Britain* (London: Hutchinson)

Marshall, G. and Swift, A. (1993) 'Social Class and Social Justice' (*British Journal of Sociology*, June)

Marshall, G. and Swift, A. (1996) 'Merit and Mobility: a reply to Peter Saunders' (*Sociology* vol. 30, no. 2)

Marsland, D. (1989) 'Universal Welfare Provision Creates a Dependent Population: The Case For' (*Soical Studies Review* Nov.)

Marx, K. (1976, first published 1867) *Capital* (Harmondsworth: Penguin)

Marx, K. and Engels, F. (1985 first published 1848) *The Communist Manifesto* (Harmondsworth: Penguin)

Matza, D. (1964) *Delinquency and Drift* (New York: Wiley)

Mayo, E. (1933) *The Human Problems of an Industrial Civilization* (New York: MacMillan)

Melton, G. (1993) 'Another Look at New Religions' (*The Annals of the American Academy of Political and Social Science* vol. 527)

Merton, R.K. (1968) *Social Theory and Social Structure* (New York: Free Press)

Mies, M. (1986) *Patriarchy and Accumulation on a World Scale: Women in the International Division of Labour* (London: Zed Press)

Miliband, R. (1969) *The State in Capitalist Society* (London: Weidenfeld and Nicolson)

Miller, W.B. (1958) 'Lower class culture as a generating milieu of gang delinquency' (*Journal of Social Issues* 14)

Miller, W.B. (1962) 'The impact of a "total community" delinquency control project' (*Social Problems* 10)

Miller, W.B. (1962) 'Lower Class Culture as a Generating Milieu of Gang Delinquency' in Wolfgang, M.E. et al. (eds.) *The Sociology of Crime and Delinquency* (New York: John Wiley and Sons)

Mills, C. W. (1956) *The Power Elite* (New York: Oxford University Press)

Mitter, S. (1995) in Mitter and Rowbotham (eds.) *Women Encounter Technology: Changing Patterns of Employment in the Third World* (London: Routledge)

Modood (1994) *Changing Ethnic Minorities* (London: PSI)

Modood, T. et al. (1997) *Fourth National Survey of Ethnic Minorities* (Policy Studies Institute)

Mosca, G. (1939) *The Ruling Class* (New York: McGraw-Hill)

Murray, C. (1984) *Losing Ground* (New York: Basic Books)

References

Murray, C. (1989) 'Underclass' (*Sunday Times Magazine* 26 Nov.)

Murray, C. (1990) *The British Underclass* (London: Institute of Economics Affairs, Health and Welfare Unit)

Murray, C. (1993) 'The Coming White Underclass' (*Wall Street Journal*, Oct. 29)

Navarro, V. (1976) *Medicine Under Capitalism* (New York: Neale Watson)

Niebuhr, H.R. (1929) *The Social Sources of Denominationalism* (New York: Holt)

Oakley, A. (1981) 'Interviewing Women: a Contradiction in Terms' in Roberts, H. (ed.) *Doing Feminist Research* (London: Routledge & Kegan Paul)

Oakley, A. (1981) *Subject Women* (London: Fontana Press)

Pakulski, J. and Waters, M. (1996) *The Death of Class* (London: Sage)

Pareto, V. (1916) A *Treatise on General Sociology* (New York: Dover)

Parsons, T. (1937) *The Structure of Social Action* (New York: McGraw-Hill)

Parsons, T. (1951) *The Social System* (New York: The Free Press)

Parsons, T. (1974) 'Religion in Postindustrial America' (*Social Research 41:2, p.193-225*)

Pearce, F. (1976) *Crimes of the Powerful* (London: Pluto Press)

Penn, R. (1985) *Skilled Workers in the Class Structure* (Cambridge: Cambridge University Press)

Popper, K. (1945) *The Open Society and its enemies* (London: Routledge)

Popper, K. (1959) *The Logic of Scientific Discovery* (London: Hutchinson)

Popper, K. (1963) *Conjectures and Refutations: The Growth of Scientific Knowledge* (London: Routledge)

Poulantzas, N. (1969) 'The Problem of the Capitalist State' (*New Left Review 58*)

Poulantzas, N. (1976) 'The Capitalist State: a Reply to Miliband and Laclau' (*New Left Review* Jan-Feb)

Redclift, M. (1987) *Sustainable Development: Exploring the Contradictions* (London: Methuen)

Reiter, H. (1989) 'Party Decline in the West: A Skeptic's View' (*Journal of Theoretical Politics*, July 1989)

Ritzer, G. (1993) *The McDonaldization of Society* (California: Pine Forge Press)

Roberts, K., Cook, F.G., Clark, S.C and Semeonoff, E. (1977) *The Fragmentary Class Structure* (London: Heinemann)

Rostow, W.W. (1971) *The Stages of Economic Growth: A Non-Communist Manifesto* (Cambridge: CUP)

Rowntree, S. (1901) *Poverty: A Study of Town Life* (London: Macmillan)

Rowntree, S. (1941) *Poverty and Progress* (London: Longman)

Rowntree, S. (1951) *Poverty and the Welfare State* (London: Longman)

Runciman, W.G. (1990) 'How many Classes are there in Contemporary British Society?' (*Sociology* vol. 24)

Saeed (1999) 'New ethnic and national questions in Scotland: post-British identities among Glasgow Pakistani teenagers' (*Ethnic and Racial Studies,* 22)

Sarlvik, B. and Crewe, I. (1983) *Decade of Dealignment* (Cambridge: CUP)

Saunders, P. (1990) *Social Class and Stratification* (London: Routledge)

Saunders, P. (1996) *Unequal but Fair? A Study of Class Barriers in Britain* (London: IEA)

Savage, M., Barlow, J., Dickens, P. and Fielding, T. (1992) *Property, Bureaucracy and Culture: Middle-class Formation in Contemporary Britain* (London: Routledge)

Savage, M. and Egerton, M. (1997) 'Social Mobility, Individual Ability and the Inheritance of Class Inequality' (*Sociology* vol. 31, no. 4)

Rt. Hon. The Lord Scarman (1981) *The Brixton Disorders, April 10-12, 1981: Inquiry Report. Chrm. Lord Scarman (Command Paper)* (London: The Stationery Office Books)

Scott, J. (1982) *The Upper Classes: Property and Privilege in Britain* (London: Macmillan)

Scott, J. (1991) *Who Rules Britain* (Cambridge: Polity Press)

Sklair, L. (1995) *Sociology of the Global System* (Hemel Hempstead: Prentice Hall)

Sklair, L. (2000) 'The Transnational Capitalist Class and the Discourse of Globalization' (*Cambridge Review of International Affairs* vol. 14, no. 1)

Snider, L. (1993) *Bad Business: Corporate Crime in Canada* (Toronto: Nelson)

Snider, L. (1993) 'Theory and Politics in the Control of Corporate Crime', in Pearce, F. and Woodiwiss, M. (eds.) *Global Crime Connections: Dynamics and Control* (London: Macmillan)

Stanworth, P. and Giddens, A. (1974) 'An Economic Elite: A Demographic Profile of Company Chairmen' in Stanworth and Giddens (eds.) *Elites and Power in British Society* (Cambridge: Cambridge University Press)

Taylor, I. Walton, P. and Young, J. (1973) *The New Criminology* (London: Routledge & Kegan Paul)

Taylor, L. (1984) *In the Underworld* (London: Unwin)

Townsend, P. (1970) *The Concept of Poverty* (London: Heinemann)

Townsend, P. (1979) *Poverty in the United Kingdom* (Harmondsworth: Penguin)

Townsend, P., Corrigan, P. and Kowarzik, U. (1987) 'Deprivation' (*Journal of Social Policy* 16)

Toynbee, P. (2003) *Hard Work: Life in Low Pay Britain* (London: Bloomsbury)

Troeltsch, E. (1931 and 1956, originally 1912) *The Social Teachings of the Christian Churches* (New York: Macmillan)

Tumin, M. (1953) 'Some Principles of Stratification: A Conceptual Analysis' (*American Sociological Review* 18)

Tumin, M. (1967) 'Some Principles of Stratification: A Critical Analysis' in Bendix, R. and Lipset, S.M. (eds.) *Social Stratification: The Forms and Functions of Social Inequality* (Englewood Cliffs, NJ: Prentice Hall)

Walby, S. (1990) *Theorising Patriarchy* (Oxford: Blackwell)

Walker, A. (1990) 'Blaming the Victims' in Murray *The Emerging British Underclass* (London: IEA)

Wallerstein, I. (1974) *The Modern World-System, Vol. I: Capitalist Agriculture and the Origins of the European World-Economy in the Sixteenth Century* (New York/London: Academic Press)

Wallerstein, I. (1980) *The Modern World-System, Vol. II: Mercantilism and the Consolidation of the European World-Economy, 1600-1750* (New York: Academic Press)

Wallerstein, I. (1989) *The Modern World-System, Vol. III: The Second Great Expansion of the Capitalist World-Economy, 1730-1840s* (San Diego: Academic Press)

Wallis, R. (1984) *The Elementary Forms of the New Religious Life* (London: Routledge & Kegan Paul)

Walsh, M. (2001) *Research Made Real: A Guide for Students* (Cheltenham: Nelson Thornes)

Weber, M. (1958) *The Protestant Work Ethic and the Spirit of Capitalism* (New York: Scribner's Sons)

Weber, M: *See also under Gerth and Mills (1948)*

Wedderburn, D. (1974) *Poverty, Inequality and Class Structure* (Cambridge: CUP)

Westergaard, J. (1995) *Who Gets What? The Hardening of Class Inequality in the Late Twentieth Century* (Cambridge, Polity Press)

Westergaard, J . and Resler, H. (1976) *Class in a Capitalist Society* (Harmondsworth: Penguin)

Whyte (1955) *Street Corner Society* (Chicago: University of Chicago)

Wilson, B. (1966) *Religion in a Secular Society* (London: C.A. Watts)

Wilson, B. (1970) *Religious Sects* (London: Weidenfeld & Nicolson)

Wilson, B. (1976) *Contemporary Transformations of Religion* (London: Oxford University Press)

Wright, E. O. (1978) *Class, Crisis and the State* (London: New Left Books)

Wright, E. O. (1985) *Classes* (London: Verso)

Wright, E. O. (1989) 'The comparative project on class structure and class consciousness: An overview' (*Acta Sociologica* Spring 32)

Wright, E. O. (1990) *The Debate on Classes* (London: Verso)

Wright, E. O. (1997) *Class Counts: Comparative Studies in Class Analysis* (Cambridge: Cambridge University Press)

Young, J. (1971) *The Drugtakers* (London: Paladin*)*

Index

Index